PENGUIN BOOKS

THE WORKING ACTOR

Katinka Matson studied acting at the Lee Strasberg Theatre Institute and the Performing Garage in New York City, where she lives and now works as a literary agent.

Judith A. Katz is a theatrical consultant to Warner Bros. east coast office. She also serves as a member of the faculty of the New School for Social Research. Ms. Katz has written about theatre and film for several publications, and is the author of *The Business of Show Business* and *The Ad Game*.

The Working Actor

A Guide to the Profession

Revised Edition

Katinka Matson and Judith Katz

PENGUIN BOOKS

PENGUIN BOOKS
Published by the Penguin Group
Penguin Books USA Inc., 375 Hudson Street,
New York, New York 10014, U.S.A.
Penguin Books Ltd, 27 Wrights Lane, London W8 5TZ, England
Penguin Books Australia Ltd, Ringwood, Victoria, Australia
Penguin Books Canada Ltd, 10 Alcorn Avenue,
Toronto, Ontario, Canada M4V 3B2
Penguin Books (N.Z.) Ltd, 182–190 Wairau Road,
Auckland 10, New Zealand

Penguin Books Ltd, Registered Offices:
Harmondsworth, Middlesex, England

First published in Penguin Books 1993

10 9 8 7 6 5 4 3 2 1

LIBRARY OF CONGRESS CATALOGING IN PUBLICATION DATA
Matson, Katinka.
The working actor : a guide to the profession / Katinka
Matson and Judith Katz.—Rev. ed.
p. cm.
ISBN 0 14 01.4433 1
1. Acting—Vocational guidance. I. Katz, Judith A.
II. Title.
PN2055.M28 1993
792'.028'023—dc20   93-12324

Printed in the United States of America
Set in Melior
Designed by Ann Gold

Preface

I knew I wanted to be an actress from the time I was in my mother's womb. —Dame Judith Anderson

People who want to become actors can be divided into two categories: those who imagine the job as a kind of fabulous fantasy that will bring them fame, fortune, and fun; and those who can't imagine doing anything else and are willing and eager to overcome any obstacle or road-block to accomplish their goal. *The Working Actor* is a book for those of you in that second category and for those of you who would like to be there.

It is our hope that by hearing the professionals in the business who hire actors and by hearing the voices of successful working actors—their thoughts, experiences, and wisdom—you will better understand what it actually takes to develop into a real working actor. You will realize that desire, talent, training, *and* an intelligent approach to your career are what will make it happen—not a fantasy or fickle chance.

Casting director Daniel Swee put it this way: "There is such an air of mystery that gets built up around the business and what happens in it that ultimately turns into a way of empowering everyone but yourself. Actors think, If only I knew an agent or a casting director, if only I'd got that audition, then I'd be a star. The truth is that an actor needs to have a good clear sense of himself and what he or she can do as an actor. He needs to be well trained, willing to work hard and to get out there and do it."

The first step in preparing yourself for a career as a working actor is to be brutally honest with yourself about your motives. Do you love the work, or the *idea* of the work? Do you have what it takes to become a working actor—talent, drive, persistence, and a very thick skin—or do you believe you are so special that surely you will be "discovered"? Are you willing to risk everything, often including parental approval and financial security, to achieve your goal?

Some people prefer not to question themselves too deeply about their motives and aspirations, but with the acting profession it is mandatory to start on firmly solid ground, with a clear understanding of the enormous and unshakable commitment it requires. Embarking upon an acting career should be treated as seriously as embarking on any other professional endeavor. And like almost everything else in life you will do better when you are prepared and ready for anything. We hope *The Working Actor* will point you in the right direction.

—Katinka Matson
Judith Katz

Contents

The Working Actor

1
Preparing Yourself

You can't depend on luck and you can't set out to become an actor in an offhanded way. Luck for an actor means putting a great amount of work and emotional commitment into something and having that come back to you in an unexpected way. —Ally Sheedy, actress

The great Russian theater director Konstantin Stanislavsky signed a copy of his book *My Life in Art* to a friend with the following inscription: "To Charles Norris Houghton, my dear comrade in art, with this friendly advice: Love the art in yourself and not yourself in art." In preparing yourself for an acting career we offer the same friendly guidance. In other words, love the *work* of acting, not just the *idea* of being an actor.

All the working actors we interviewed for this book had one thing in common: their decision to become actors came from a desire to do the work. Their accomplishments came from an intelligent approach to their careers and a fervent belief in their own talent.

As a young actor today you too will need to develop a realistic approach to your career because simply saying you're an actor isn't enough. You will have to earn that right. How? First, by training. If there is one current trend in the acting profession it is that now more than ever before actors are required to be well trained, preferably at a prestigious conservatory like Juilliard or a graduate school like Yale. Secondly, you will need theatre experience, even if you dream of movie-stardom. And finally, to earn the right to call yourself an actor you must have an ironclad belief in your own talent, a healthy and professional attitude toward rejection, and a comprehensive knowledge of the business you wish to be a part of, including a keen perception of how you fit in.

Like anything worthwhile, a solid approach is built through process and experience. Experience and knowledge come out of experimentation, trial and error. In the following section, you will learn from working actors, in their own voices, how they got started and what philosophy sustained them.

We all know about the glamorous aspects of an actor's life—the premieres, the awards, the recognition—because that is the part we see. But actors, particularly beginning actors, must live an attentive, diligent, and observant life to come out on top, or risk being left with a fantasy rather than an acting career. Everything you learn about the business, especially how professionals think, will be helpful and pay off sooner or later. Awareness leads you in the right direction and teaches you how to present yourself as an actor in an appropriate way. Lack of awareness leads you into dreamland and that old joke:

> Q: What do you do?
> A: I'm an actor.
> Q: Oh, really? Which restaurant?

VOICES

B. D. Wong

B. D. Wong's love and enthusiasm for acting carried him from a seventeen-year-old hopeful to a formidable role in Broadway's M. Butterfly and a solid career in theatre, movies, and television.

"I grew up in San Francisco. In the third or fourth grade I was encouraged to study the violin privately because I had potential. I began to study very seriously, but by the ninth grade I realized I had no interest in the violin. At a transitional point I decided to play in the orchestra for a school musical because I wanted to be involved somehow and playing an instrument was what I could do. I had a friend who said, 'Why don't you be in the play instead?' I wanted to, but I needed someone else to make me do it. I was afraid; I thought the others would laugh at me for wanting to be an actor. I accompanied my friend to the audition. I found the auditioning process interesting and found myself being quite competitive even though I had no experience with this kind of thing. The play was *Guys and Dolls*. I remember fighting for the little parts and really being disappointed that I didn't get one of the principal roles. The teacher saw I was enthusiastic so she gave me a lot of different small roles. I assembled quite a role for myself by threading together all these parts.

"So I became involved in the play and as soon as I was on the stage I realized there was something here I was connecting with. Here was something I could contribute to and could also get something out of. The teacher took a liking to me and eventually she became my mentor. And

I got bigger parts the next time around and more parts and then I started doing community theatre.

"Immediately after doing that first ninth-grade play I auditioned with a group of friends for a summer community theatre in San Francisco. Theatre was an obsession for me and clearly something I preferred to schoolwork, but none of my family could see how it related to real life. So, of course, my parents were concerned. If someone you loved became obsessed with whittling you'd be concerned in the same way, because what value would it have for their life? So at the earliest stage no one could imagine that I would become a professional actor. They felt it was a whim and a waste of time.

"The following summer I got involved in a semiprofessional production and that really whetted my appetite. I got paid and could compete with professional actors. But I wasn't looking to earn a living, I was looking to just be in a show. And I could do that at San Francisco University, San Francisco State, summer stock and community theatre. And I did all of those things. I was also completely involved in my high school senior project, How to Succeed in Business Without Really Trying. Sometime during that time period I started to say I can't think of anything else I would rather do. Also during that time my parents had an evolution and saw my potential and my enthusiasm, which was not like other people's—it was gargantuan and monstrous in a positive way. They began to believe that maybe I should explore acting as a possibility.

"Shortly after high school I was hired by the San Francisco school district to be a director of theatre in public schools. That was extremely rewarding. I was going to San Francisco State, but I was not enjoying it. I wanted to come to New York.

"While I was directing the school plays I was also a part-time bank teller, a cookie-maker at Mrs. Fields Cookies, and a volunteer usher so I could see all the great theatre. I lived with my parents and saved every single penny.

"I came to New York with all my savings. I was nineteen years old. Before I left I asked everybody I knew who had been to New York to tell me everything they knew about it. I was told about the freezing weather, that I had to have a lot of money and had to be careful about where I lived —and I had to expect it would not be easy. Before I came, throughout my entire schooling, I was counseled that being an actor was almost impossible for an Asian-American. I digested all this the way I digest most challenges: I often take the opposite view because I want to accept a challenge. It was mostly relatives, not my parents, who said there isn't much opportunity. They couldn't believe I would quit my job as an usher to try and do what actors do. They gave me a party before I left, but you could feel the doom they felt for me.

"I was always somebody who didn't fit in, but I didn't see any point in allowing that to bother me. Much of this had to do with what my parents taught me—don't react when somebody rejects you. That and the fact that I was fueled with so much enthusiasm allowed me to turn away from an audition and say to myself, Well, okay, where is the next audition? My parents were fantastic and are responsible for what I enjoy now. They can really share with me what I reap. They suppressed all their natural parental fear, and remember, they are not progressive Berkeley liberals but first- and second-generation Chinese-Americans. My older brother is a doctor and my younger brother a firefighter; they encouraged us to forge ahead in individuality.

"When I was in New York I would call my parents after blowing an audition and they would say 'Don't worry about it, just keep trying.' Obviously I was passed over

many more times than I was hired—that's the way it is—
but they always said 'Don't worry, don't give up.' That
response always surprised me and it was incredibly helpful. There are thousands of people out there who will not
have parents like mine. They shouldn't think that they are
unfortunate because they don't have this kind of support.
The main thing is to estabish a support system of your
own, with people that you can turn to when you need to
vent or express disappointment and frustration. Having
people there to help me cope and sustain myself was very
important to me.

"I got my pictures taken soon after coming to New York.
I knew good pictures were important; so was a résumé. I
was very compulsive about presenting my limited experience in a professional manner. I constantly read *Backstage* and I constantly went to auditions even if I wasn't
right for the role because I wanted to become comfortable
with the audition process. I wanted to learn how to open
the door.

"I didn't think twice about getting up at six in the morning. That was all part of an exciting thing to me, it really
was fun. I went to audition every day, sometimes twice a
day. Some people don't agree with me, but I believe auditioning is the only way to learn how to audition. So why
not just go out there and audition even if you're not meant
for the role. At the beginning, auditioning is not about
career decisions—it is about going into a room and being
able to pick up a piece of paper and read it for someone
else.

"I came to New York in January of 1982. By Valentine's
Day I got my first job. It was in a children's theatre production of a rock musical. Someone had told me to go and
audition for children's theatre because everyone was out
of town looking for work for the spring. It turned out to
be true. But if you had read the breakdown you would not

have encouraged me to go to the audition. I had no agent at the time—I was told I didn't need one in New York, especially because I was aiming myself for a career in musical theater on Broadway. I went on chorus line auditions all the time. Of course I wanted speaking parts, but I would have taken anything. My second job was in a dinner theatre in Ohio. A funny thing happened during that time: just before I got my Equity card I was hired for five different jobs in non-Equity productions. I had to turn them all down because I got my card.

"There was a point after I came to New York, in 1983, when it seemed to me that nothing was happening, there was much less activity than when I first arrived. I had also grown out of a certain kind of interview. I wanted speaking parts. So I decided to go to Los Angeles. I learned how to audition there. I got myself an agent there. That wasn't hard for me because I went immediately to an agency that handles Asian actors, the Bessie Lou Agency. I was sent up for a lot of things. I got to read for movies and television shows, so the auditions seemed more legitimate.

"Auditions were different in Los Angeles because I was in a different pool of actors. I was no longer singing, I was acting. But I soon realized I couldn't compete with actors of caliber—something I very much wanted to do—unless I studied and pushed myself to learn as much as I could every day. In New York I never took professional classes. I came out of a situation where I was the star of my high school and a lot of people, like my high school teacher/mentor, encouraged me to go for it. So it never occurred to me how spoiled I had become with all the positive reception I was getting in high school. I didn't realize the value of study then, or really until I came to Los Angeles and started to audition for speaking roles.

"Also, classes forced me not to be lazy. L.A. is such a beautiful and pleasant place to live, it is tempting to go to the beach every day. In the middle of my time in L.A. I went through a brief lazy period. I'd say to myself, My big break is going to come along, but there are no auditions today so I think I'll go to the beach, eventually an audition will come along and I'll be really good at it and I'll probably get the part and become a star.

"I soon realized that that attitude doesn't work because you have to be ready for it to happen. You can become so complacent the opportunities will zip right by you. Early on I thought talent was all I needed. Also, I was a good and moral person, so karmically I didn't see why it shouldn't happen for me. I found an acting teacher through a recommendation, Don Hotten, who worked with six or seven other students in his living room. I didn't want an academy or a big school. I didn't know exactly what my limitations were but I wanted to learn a technique and hone my skills. And I started working with a voice teacher. I was a good singer but had major vocal limitations.

"Studying gave me much higher self-esteem because I was investing in my future on a daily basis. I started getting auditions again and I got a really good part in a television movie. As soon as that happened I realized that my philosophy really worked. Investing energy, time, and money in myself really worked. More opportunity came to me and I was more able to handle the audition opportunities when they came.

"I was doing well in Los Angeles when in March 1987 an agent called to say that David Henry Hwang had written a play and would I be interested in coming to New York to audition? I wasn't starving in L.A. and I thought it wasn't sensible for me to pack up and go back to New York, so I asked how big was the part, is it planned for Broadway, what is it about. I said it would be nice if I could read the script. He called back and said yes, it was a big part and it was for Broadway, but I would have to fly myself back for the audition. I said, 'I don't think I want to do that, but send me the script.' That was on a Friday and the script came on Monday.

"I read about half of M. Butterfly and realized I had to go. But I didn't have the money. So I called my folks and told them that I had to fly to New York to audition. I said I was almost certain I won't get the part but I cannot pass up the opportunity to read for this play. I asked them to send me the money.

"You never know whether you really are going to get a part because you don't know the variables that could keep you from getting it. The reason I picked up the phone to call in the first place is because I knew I had something inside me that would allow me to play the part. So I called my folks and they sent me the money to go to New York. They were funny about it, but they trusted my judgment.

"I went to New York on that Thursday and read for them. I auditioned once, had breakfast with the director, John Dexter, the next day to talk about the part. I was told a lot of guys had read for the part but not a lot of guys were up for it. After breakfast he told me to come back in June—that was in March. I was glad for the opportunity to have time to work on the part because I only had two days for this first audition.

"When they called in June I was doing another play at the Pasadena Playhouse. This time I insisted that they pay for me to fly in. I read the second time—on a Tuesday. I was given the part that Thursday. I had great pride in the fact that I got the part, but also that I did the right thing. That I didn't say, Oh, gee, it's thousands of miles away and I'm not going to get the role so why bother.

"I'm happy with my life because I have seldom copped out and said I can't do that so I won't try. I never found value in being negative. I think negativity gets in a lot of actors' ways. I'd come across actors at Equity's lounge in

New York who would complain about not getting parts. Certainly there is a problem for unknown actors to get seen, but time spent in the lounge complaining could be spent taking a class or auditioning or something—when you really have the calling, the passion, you make the most of your time.

"Asian actors have a bone to pick with society for the lack of roles for us—it is a symptom of what is wrong with society in general. I like thinking about how I can be a part of changing that condition. I played the role of a reporter in a TV movie about racism in Boston. In the original script my character never commented on the issue. I told the producers an Asian-American would certainly comment on such a highly inflammatory racial situation. They wrote a new scene for me. I was proud of that. Instead of saying nothing, or turning the part down, I got them to change it."

On Advice to Young Actors

"There is a controversy among actors about what kind of advice to give kids who want to be actors. Some say don't do it, just don't. I find that response shocking. As an actor who is now experiencing the joy of acting and validation from the audience, I don't see why young people are not encouraged to become actors. The glorious feelings I have now that I've traveled part of the road justifies the toils. But I don't encourage people who decide to try acting after they have tried lots of other things. To me that indicates a lack of passion and commitment. You can't be an actor just by wanting to be one. You have to really need it, want it, and know it. We think we want a lot of things in life, so you have to be careful in figuring out if you really want to be an actor. How I knew was that acting was the only thing I ever experienced in life that I could give to and get back from; I can contribute to the art form and I draw enormous pleasure from it.

"Learning how to be an actor is not merely learning information. It is learning information and incorporating it with something inside of you. So obviously some ingredients need to be inside you. The ingredient which most interests me is the need to breathe life into the words of great writers. I encourage actors who have a voice and want to say things, as opposed to actors who only want to make money. I don't condone acting as an everyday, commonplace profession. Actors show us what is inside us, our shortcomings, teach us how to be better, how society can improve. Everyone, not only actors, should decide what to become based on what they can do that will serve society. Not that there is anything wrong with wanting to be a movie star—I want to be one, too. But I want to be one so that I can represent fine writers like David Henry Hwang.

"You have to be willing to take risks as an actor. But there is a big difference between putting yourself on the line, gambling and playing your hunches, and being stupid, not thinking clearly or using forethought. Finding yourself in New York your second week with no money is stupid. Expecting to go to auditions without a picture and résumé is not smart. Before you set out to become a professional actor, you need to know as much as possible about the life of a professional actor and realize that you can't stop studying and trying to improve your craft. A large part of your money should go towards that. You are the product. If you were trying to sell a car, you would polish it to make sure it looks good, you would make sure the parts were well oiled and ready to go when you need them to. In the same way, you have to take care of yourself as an actor. You have to be healthy, presentable, clear-headed and strong. You have to find a supportive community, if not from your parents then from friends—real friends are vital. It helps to have feedback about your work, your demeanor, even your haircut from someone you trust and respect. And you have to be as good as you can be."

Ally Sheedy

We first met Ally Sheedy at a movie screening she was attending with her mother. Ally was twelve years old and curious about the first edition of this book, because she said she was going to be an actress. There were no ifs, ands, or buts about it. Such invincible determination from a twelve-year-old made a strong impression on us and we weren't surprised to see Ally a few years later in a Mc-Donald's commercial. We asked her how she went from being a determined twelve-year-old who said "I'm going to be an actress" to actually becoming one.

"When I was little I wanted to be a ballerina, so I started training in dance with American Ballet Theatre. I loved being onstage and I loved telling stories and I began to think I wanted to act. I grew up in New York, so I went to see a lot of plays. Theatre was an important influence on me; we didn't watch a lot of television in my house. When I was fourteen I enrolled myself in the Neighborhood Playhouse in New York. I had written a book, which came out when I was twelve, and I made some money from it, so I used that money for my acting classes because my parents didn't want me to study acting. Neighborhood Playhouse had a junior theatre school, so I went over and auditioned. I went all through high school, every weekend, and I loved it. Then I started doing all the plays in high school. At night I would volunteer to work in all these small theatres in the city. I worked as an assistant stage manager, prop person, wardrobe—anything, just to be around and watch the actors every night. I remember one job I had when I was thirteen . . . I was the person who stood backstage and had to catch the things people threw offstage. It was a raucous musical and the lead actor was always trying to fake me out. But I got to listen to the actors talk. It was great. In class on weekends I did the exercises and scene work and during the week at night I was working backstage on a play and watching working actors actually using the skills that I was just beginning to learn.

"When I was fifteen I found a manager, and she set me up with commercial agents and eventually a theatrical agent. I did a lot of commercials. I don't like auditioning for parts—I find that taxing and hard even now—but I liked auditioning for commercials and actually working. I was still in high school, so I loved meeting people and learning what they did for a living. I liked learning about the cameras and lights. I even thought to myself then that this is great training if I'm ever going to be in the movies because I can get comfortable with the equipment. I got that attitude from my family—to take a situation and figure out how to use it.

"I did commercials for four years, all through high school. Every summer I would study at a different school. Juilliard had a summer program then and one year I did apprentice work upstate with the Acting Company summer program. I got into USC's drama department, which seemed like a good program to me and it was in California, where I wanted to go. Also, I wanted to keep working while I was in school and I wanted to work in movies; both of those were a possibility at USC so I went out there that summer. My manager was opening an L.A. office so I went out with someone from her office. Neither of us knew anyone in Hollywood. I was excited and believed it was going to work out.

"After I signed with my agent they started sending me out on auditons. I was working as a waitress and also going to USC. My first job was in an "Afterschool Special" starring Jennifer Jason Leigh, who is now a friend. Then I got little parts on movies-of-the-week and a pilot. Just getting a line here and a small part there offered me a lot to learn. But at least I wasn't overwhelmed because I was familiar with the equipment and with the audition process—walking into a room and reading lines. Also, I had been in class all that time, in New York and then in L.A. I didn't feel like I was sitting around languishing, waiting to get a part; I was working on it. My movie career really started when I was nineteen, after four years of working professionally, when I got the part in *Bad Boys*.

"I went in and read for it one day right after school. I was in my jeans and had no makeup on. Sean Penn was the lead and he read with me. After I read they asked me to come back and wear a dress or something. So I came back wearing a dress. I read the scene and then they had me stand there and talk to Sean. I think the reason I got the part is because he was really sweet. He took out a cigarette and matchbook and did this kind of magic trick while they were taping the audition and it was such a cool, funny trick it made me laugh, loosened me up, and I got the part. After that we started filming. I auditioned for *WarGames* at the same time. At the *WarGames* audition I first met Rob Lowe. All the people that are out there now were all starting to audition then. The actors who were really sticking with it, those faces you'd see at auditions all the time: Demi Moore, Rob Lowe, Eric Stoltz, Emilio Estevez, were all auditioning when I was. After a while, we all made the transition and began working. It was like a graduating class.

"I auditioned for *WarGames* for four months, almost every week. I didn't know if I was going to get the part, but I just kept showing up every time they called. Once I went in on a Saturday for an open call for the guys. Finally I got it. They had decided on Matthew Broderick and they liked the chemistry between us on a tape they made. I could have given the greatest reading in the world, but if that didn't exist I wouldn't have gotten the part. A lot of times it just has to do with how you fit with who else is in the movie.

"I think the difference between actors who stick with it and those who disappear is a willingness to take risks. Actually, you have to be willing to risk everything that is secure in your life. If you live somewhere where there aren't a lot of things going on, you have to leave and go where the work is. Every time you audition for something you take a risk, even an audition for an acting class. You have to show up and keep working on it, and if you don't get in the first time, then you keep auditioning until eventually you do. You have to be able to get up in front of everybody and fall on your face. You have to keep falling on your face—that's a big part of it.

"What sustained me was my knowing absolutely that this is what I wanted to do. When I am acting it feels right and I trust that feeling more than I trust anybody's opinion of what I do. Even if I went in for 150 auditions and wasn't right for any of them, I still knew and know that when I'm showing up, I'm happy—whether it is a class or a job—it feels right. It is hard, but I love it. That is the reason I want to act.

"Being a successful actor can be really difficult and having lots of failure can be very difficult. The results of an acting career are always going in one direction or another and you never know how you are going to react. The thing that is constant is that love, the one thing I hope I never lose."

On Advice to Young Actors

"If you want to be an actor, you have to love it more than anything else in the world. That is the only way you are going to stick with it considering the incredible adventure you'll have and the pain that is involved. Like a dancer who often has to go on with a broken toe, an actor often has to keep going with a broken ego. You probably won't find out if you love acting until you actually go out and start doing it. If you find you do love it and want to do it, then your heart is going to get you there. It will be apparent to you that this is where you belong.

"Like musicians, actors also inherit a style of living along with a job. It is a world that you should willingly agree to enter, because it is a difficult world with a lot of history to it. This may sound strange, but there was a time in history when plays and even actors were considered a religious rite. People would go to the theatre and have revelations about themselves or God. Well, in some ways that is still true. Audiences have an emotional response to actors; they love you or hate you or want to be like you.

"Acting is not something you do from nine to five and then go home and shut the door. There isn't a way to separate your life from your work. It takes over your life. It is the strangest job in the world. You travel most of the time. You always have some character living in your head and your body that isn't you. You have somebody else's words that you are thinking about, somebody else's emotions to deal with, and that can be uncomfortable because it is difficult to separate your own emotions from a character's. And you are always being judged, an audience is always watching you.

"I think you have to be a little crazy to be an actor. You live life to the fullest but you take so many chances and go through so much pain as well as joy. It is always extreme. That is the legacy you inherit. You have to learn to cope, especially if you are a successful actor. Being a successful actor is a very strange sort of thing to be. I find I tend to gravitate towards other actors who are going through the same things I am. They understand that to have a part in a popular movie is wonderful and brings you a lot of attention, but that success can turn its back on you. Suddenly the question is, How are you going to top this? or, Is your next movie going to make as much money? or, How much did you have to do with making the movie popular? All this stuff that has nothing to do with the actual experience of acting. It can be a frightening, scary place to be.

"The more you work, the more you realize that acting is a career with huge highs and tremendous lows. I've gotten tons of advice from people who say you just endure, you just keeping loving it and you just keep at it no matter what. You have to love acting, and the roles you play in movies that flop as much as the roles you play in movies that succeed. You have to love the process, not just the results."

Jason Alexander

Jason Alexander has worked in theatre, film, television, and radio, and won a Tony Award in Jerome Robbins' Broadway. He is best known for his role as George Costanza in NBC's "Seinfeld." But at the start of his career he didn't really fit into an existing mold, a problem faced by many talented actors.

"After my bar mitzvah I realized that I wanted to be an actor. It was fairly easy, I got top billing, made a lot of money for a three-hour gig, and got lots of kudos! I can do this, I said to myself. I had been in school plays, but after my bar mitzvah I started asking about voice lessons and dance lessons. At first I studied voice with the cantor of my temple and dance with two little old ladies at the Whipple School of Dance in West Orange, New Jersey— I was the only boy in class.

"Then I did children's theatre, community theatre, high school theatre. I did my first job for AFTRA [American Federation of Television and Radio Artists] when I was seventeen. A little community theatre in New Jersey had gotten a grant from PBS to film two of their plays as a television pilot. In the middle of rehearsals one of the actors got a role in a Broadway show and they needed someone to put in his role fast. The actor who needed to be replaced had been a judge in a high school talent contest I had been in and he knew I was a quick study, so he recommended me and I was hired.

"The pilot wasn't picked up by PBS, but it was aired as a children's show on a local CBS station. A woman who knew me when I was a little kid—I worked on some children's theatre with her—called to say she had recently become a manager and asked me if I would like to be a client. She asked me to sign a three-year contract with her and I decided I had nothing to lose. I knew I was going to college anyway, so if worse came to worse I wouldn't work while I was in school.

"I went to Boston University and was an acting major. All during college I free-lanced with about a dozen New York agents through my manager and ended up getting a lot of commercial work. I never finished college because during the summer of my junior year I got a part in a horror movie. The film went about two weeks over schedule, so I had to miss the first two weeks of school. I thought I could make up the two weeks, but the administration said come back next semester. I never did.

"After I left school I didn't want to go home to live so I went to work for the casting director who had cast me in that horror movie. But it was never a question of whether or not I was going to be an actor. I kept thinking, I am an actor. I am an actor. Maybe that is why I have a career today. I always thought of myself as an actor.

"By the time I left school I was a member of every union, I had commercial credits, and I had these managers, which was very important because I needed someone to help me. I was a weird type—twenty years old but with a maturity that made me seem older. I had already started losing my hair, I was overweight, I was a strange type. John Belushi was just coming into vogue at that point and no one had seen anything like him before. And here I was—a younger version of Belushi but I didn't do 'gross out' stuff. I was not that type either. So no one knew what to do with me. But my managers said, 'This kid is good.' They just popped me from agent to agent and I got in sometimes and auditioned.

"Then I met a teacher who said things to me that really made sense. He told me point-blank, 'I'll change your career in a year,' and that's exactly what he did. He taught me how to audition, and because I learned how to audition I got jobs. Because I got jobs, I got to audition more and it became a cycle. It is a lot easier when the people you are auditioning for are people you've met before rather than an unknown person judging you out there in the dark.

"I started going to auditions with a 'We're gonna have fun' attitude. I'm a sorta funny guy, so I used that. Because I was a very heavy kid when I was young I was always entertaining other kids—I think probably to distract them from the fact—so I had a full repertoire of jokes and stories. I know actors who can't work unless it is out of agony and pain. But really this isn't life-and-death stuff, it's a play or a movie.

"My first Broadway show, *Merrily We Roll Along*, was a disaster. I was out of work for ten months after that, and then all hell broke loose for me commercially. In the course of the following year I did twenty national commercials. Before that, if I had three national commercials I felt I was making a living. The best known was for Western Union—one of their 'Keep in Touch' spots. Commercials made up the bulk of my living. And, of course, I continued doing theatre, which I could afford to do because of the commercials.

"My career has been unusual in that I haven't had to claw and scratch and bite and fight because I always had people helping me. I adored my managers. They launched my career and it would not have happened the way it did without them. No agent would commit to me back then, but my managers would watch the breakdowns and say I could do this or that job and they would badger every poor agent in town. That is what a manager at their level does—they have relationships with all these agents.

"After a while, as I got a little older and grew into my type, I had a résumé and people knew who I was, then agents wanted me. So my managers' next job was to hook me up with a really good agent, which they did.

"When I was twenty-four my agent got a breakdown for a role in a TV movie described as a forty- to forty-five-year-old ethnic police lieutenant. She said, 'You could do this,' called the casting director, and got me in. I went to the audition thinking, I'll never get this so I might as well act the shit out of the part—do what Broderick Crawford would do with this part. I got it. They just said 'Let's go this way . . . Here is someone a little out of the ordinary, let's have some fun.' From that experience I learned to do every audition as if I could get it, but not to go in there saying God, I can taste this, this is the one. Even if I felt I may be wrong for a part, I tried never to take that feeling into the room but have fun with it instead.

"There is a difference between being able to do any

kind of a role and being acceptable at it. I am able to *play* a gorgeous leading man, but I'm not acceptable playing a gorgeous leading man. I can act like a man who has a history of charming women, who has that quality, but I'm not going to get Sean Connery roles—his masculinity is a different sort of thing. But I could play a sexy role as long as I know what quality about me women find attractive. Brian Dennehy discovered what makes him attractive to women and women loved him in *Cocoon* despite his being overweight and not traditionally handsome.

"Movies were tough for me before *Pretty Woman*, even after *Jerome Robbins' Broadway*. The only reason I got *Pretty Woman* was because Richard Gere and the casting director went to bat for me. They were looking at people more on the money. The director said no and was adamant about it."

On Advice to Young Actors

"If there is anything else you can do and be reasonably happy—not even ecstatically happy—do it. If you can't be reasonably happy doing something else, then you will do fine.

"Because of my own experience I always tell actors to start early. I never went through the transition of being a student to being someone who was trying to get a job. The time periods overlapped so I never had those moments of wondering, How do I do this? I just did it.

"I went to school with students who were amazing actors. If you lined us up on a stage and told us all to act, no one would look at me. Yet they can't get a break because they don't have someone to help them, or they don't audition enough, or both. When they do get a shot it means life or death for them, so they can't present themselves in an appealing way. What you see is someone sitting there saying 'I need this,' and that is intimidating to a casting director.

"It is difficult to get into any auditions of merit without help. If you are having trouble getting an agent, I think going with a good manager is not a bad route. I would suggest, however, that before signing with a manager you learn which agents they work with and who their other clients are, otherwise you could sign with managers who aren't able to earn their percentage.

"Study everything you possibly can and watch other actors. Just like a writer, a painter, a musician, there are skills to this profession, tools and ways to work that you have to know. Unless you know them, you are limited. If you are limited as an actor, you are dead."

James McDaniel

The realities of pursuing a career in acting are harsher for some actors than for others. For instance, there are fewer roles for women than there are for men. Another inequity is that there are fewer roles for minority actors. James McDaniel is an African-American who faced this challenge and went on to become a Broadway actor and recently co-starred with Stephen Rea of The Crying Game in the play Someone Who'll Watch Over Me.

"I had no plans to be an actor. I was studying to be a veterinarian at the University of Pennsylvania and at a party one night a friend said to me, 'You're an actor.' And it hit me like a thunderbolt because I knew that I was an actor but had squashed my ambitions and given myself the role of the little scientist in the family. My sister was an actress and had gone to Boston University and the London Academy. So I went to vet school but realized it was the furthest thing away from what I wanted to do or could do. I left school and came to New York.

"I didn't know anything about acting. I had been in one school play. I had six hundred dollars to my name, so I moved into a Y and started taking dance classes immediately. There was a small talent agency attached to the dance studio and this woman begged me for a picture. I didn't have any pictures so I asked a friend to take a snapshot and blew it up. She sent me on an audition for a Pepsi commercial and I booked it. My first commercial audition!

"The commercial was the first 'Hero' spot and won all kinds of awards and was played all over the world forever, so I was making a hell of a lot of money. And I used it to study. I just kept on studying—here and there. I studied at HB Studio with Steve Strimpel, then I went uptown and studied with Ernie McClintock, and then I studied with Earl Hyman. I did a lot of little snatches with different people. But my real studying began when I did a play called *A Soldier's Play* and something happened.

"The play was a big hit and one of the actors who had done real well in the show had to leave suddenly because his father died. They had to get someone in quick and it wasn't an easy role to cast. The part called for someone who could play the guitar. I had put guitar and singing on my résumé, and they were leafing through in this frantic search for somebody, anybody, to cover this guy, so they auditioned me and hired me because they had to hire me. And I did the job. I got it done. The play was produced at the Negro Ensemble Company. Later it was made into a movie called *A Soldier's Story*.

"That is when my professional career started moving and that is where my studying led to. People came and saw me. Suddenly I had an agent. Then I was doing a lot of plays, which is exactly what I wanted to do. I remember one night my agent came to see me and he said, 'What are you going to do now, are we going to make a lot of money this year?' I said, 'No, I want to do five plays a year for the next five years.'

"When I got the role of Paul 'Poitier' in Six Degrees of Separation things really started to happen. But it is funny, people would say 'Wow, where did this new guy come from?' But they saw me five times a year, as a cop, a thug, a lawyer. But Six Degrees had a certain amount of prestige and all of a sudden I was validated. But it had been ten years between A Soldier's Play and Six Degrees of Separation.

"I chased Six Degrees with a vengeance for nine months. I would have been crushed had I not gotten it. Jerry Zaks is very exacting and auditions more thoroughly than any director I've ever worked with. Our auditions lasted an hour, sometimes two hours. We'd read the whole play and then certain sections over again. We worked three lines twenty times, and each time he would give me another adjustment. He called me back at least five times and would have called me back again, but I had to give him sort of an ultimatum. I was going broke waiting for this show and I had gotten another offer that looked really good.

"I called Jerry to say that it was nice working with him and maybe at some other time we would be able to work together, but I had to take another job. We talked for about forty-five minutes and hung up. About fifteen minutes later my agent called and told me that I had the job.

"I saw the genius of Six Degrees from the second I read the first page. You had to appreciate the fact that here was a role like none before. It was a very large character, right in the center of everything, and it was antagonistic.

"Everyone always says that there are too many stereotypical roles for blacks. I think there are too few because, let's face it, most roles are stereotypical. It is an actor's job to put a spin on a role, to make the character intellectual, or intriguing, or sexy. White actors get more opportunity to play with subtlety because they have a wide range of characters. There are, perhaps, four different roles written for us: the pimp; the junkie; the prostitute; the straight, bland, corny guy. If they would create more so-called stereotypes there would be more roles for black actors. I don't want to play a junkie if all they have me doing is laying in a corner with a needle in my arm, but if I could get down into what being a junkie is all about, what makes a human being become that thing, that would be a different matter. There is always something to discover in a character that you want to say. I once played a Rastafarian in a play. I didn't know much about Rastafarians, but I got into the character's head so much that I had a real need to correct the misconceptions about them. That is what acting is for me.

"All actors, black and white, have to open up the floodgates and do whatever the character needs to have done. I did an episode of 'L.A. Law' in which I played an army attorney who won a case against Susan Dey. The director thought I was playing a particular scene too hard. I asked him, Why is it inappropriate for me to be hard in the scene or do you mean you want people to like me? He admitted he just wanted some leeway in there for the audience to like the black guy. Well, I don't want to be boxed into a situation like that and I told him.

"I went into Six Degrees with a preexisting contract for 'Cop Rock,' so I had to leave before the end of the run. 'Cop Rock' was a Steven Bochco project, was very ambitious. It was a challenge to cast, but they put together a great ensemble. Everybody meshed, we were all theatre actors so we spoke the same language. It was disappointing when the show was canceled. But I look at my forebears and I say, My great grandfather was hung from a tree, my father had to go through all sorts of things to achieve what he did, so who am I to feel down about anything? I take what I've got and I try to make it better. What else can I do? Pack my bags? We are all stuck with some disappointments; maybe they will take us someplace better. And who knows—then maybe we'll just blow the roof off the sucker!"

On Advice to Young Actors

"Investigate your motives for wanting to come into the business. If you think you are doing it for glamour and fame, there are a hell of a lot of other easier ways to be glamorous and famous. But if you can honestly say that you have a desire to put out your point of view, then I think this is a great business to go into.

"Take yourself seriously. I never ever thought that I was being silly, that this was possibly not what I should be doing with my life. There's a lot of waiting involved and you need patience. You've got to have faith in yourself.

"Learn your craft. Acting is hard work. There is no such thing as natural talent as far as I'm concerned, unless you are talking about doing triple pirouettes or even looking good. Acting talent is an ability to focus in a certain direction. You've just got to get into it and then put it out there.

"Go everywhere, see everything, and experience all you can. And be hard on the professionals you are going to encounter because there are a lot of people out there selling stuff to actors that is just not applicable. Get the real story."

Jane Adams

For several years, Jane Adams struggled with the dilemma of going to Juilliard or going directly into the New York

*job market. Professionals she respected offered a kalei-
doscope of advice. After much reflection, conservatory
training seemed to make the most sense, but the conflict
remained with her throughout her schooling. It wasn't
until two years after she graduated that she realized the
benefits she gained by being cloistered for four years in a
world of theatre. In addition to working off Broadway,
Jane has co-starred on Broadway in Paul Rudnick's I Hate
Hamlet and appeared as Michael J. Fox's girlfriend in
"Family Ties."*

"I was Pinocchio in my sixth-grade play and from that
point on I always wanted to be in the school plays. Then
I decided I wanted to be a painter. In college I studied
political science. But acting is always where I ended up.
I grew up in Wheaton, Illinois, but my family moved to
Seattle and I went to high school and college there. There
is a lot of theatre going on in Seattle. I was still in school
when I got my first job in an Equity production and joined
Equity.

"I acted for a year in Seattle, going from one play to the
next. It was relatively easy for me there—I had become
the Seattle ingenue. Since I lived there I was always available. But I knew I wanted to live and work in New York.

"One of the plays I did at the Seattle Rep was seen by
the producers of Playwrights Horizons, who wanted to
bring the play to New York the following April. They said
they would like to use me if they did, but that was a year
away. I was twenty-one at the time and didn't really know
what I was going to do with the rest of my life.

"An associate director at Seattle Rep said I should go
to Juilliard; the other director said I shouldn't go; a third
told me to just keep working and forget about long-term
training. I was very conflicted. It wasn't a new conflict—
all during the time I was in college I asked myself if after

I graduated I should get out there and struggle or go to graduate school.

"On the one hand I thought working begets more work, and ultimately that is what I was after. And Juilliard puts a hold on working for a long time—four years *is* a long time, especially since I was playing young women. Yale is only three years. On the other hand, my big dream then was to be a working actress in an off-Broadway play in New York.

"I decided to audition for Juilliard. My parents were happy about it because it seemed like something concrete and I felt that way, too. I called Juilliard, but they said it was too late. I said, 'I'm going to audition, just tell me where I have to go.' The woman told me that there was an audition in San Francisco, but it was the very next day. So I bought a ticket to fly down.

"On the way to the airport, a friend told me about another friend who had also auditioned for Juilliard and had gotten in. My friend said this other actor told himself, 'I'm going to Juilliard,' not 'I'm auditioning,' but 'I'm going.' So I said, 'I'm going to Juilliard.' And it sort of changed the whole experience for me. I auditioned and got in.

"At the end of my first year Playwrights Horizons did decide to produce that play I was in in Seattle and I was offered the part. But Juilliard had a policy of not allowing students to work while they are studying. They are right to do this, but the play was an important opportunity for me. One of the teachers went to bat for me and I was allowed to do the play. The play wasn't a success, but Harry Abrams, the agent, liked me and signed me, so I got my first agent as a result.

"Having an agent while I was in school caused problems. I'd get offers for jobs I couldn't accept and sometimes I felt tremendous pressure. I felt I had to do whatever I had to do to insure I'd be able to start working when I got out of school, but I didn't want to leave school. Making it work financially was difficult for me. I had scholarships and loans, but Juilliard didn't have dormitories then (they do now), and I didn't want to move out of Manhattan.

"Looking back on my years at Juilliard I realize how much I was able to accomplish there. You are completely immersed in the experience. You can't go to Juilliard for training without being affected as a person. You make a huge commitment and spend all this time, so you come out a different person. It was a real emotional experience, very difficult for me. Still, I learned a lot.

"Every day you learn how much you don't know. It can be tricky, because in the beginning you lose confidence, but then somehow you get it back—it all comes together. Juilliard doesn't really teach one method. You are inundated with every different way to approach a script and develop a character. Everything is thrown at you. That is the wonderful part of the training, because afterwards you are prepared for any kind of situation. The thing about long-term training, especially Juilliard, is that you have to find a way of maintaining your own identity and at the same time take it all in. The danger is in letting go so much that you forget what you brought into the program in the first place.

"I especially liked the mask class. You put on these stark white masks, they are different characters, like maybe an old woman. The masks seem to give people the freedom to become someone else.

"We didn't do a lot of plays. They do more plays at Yale. And we didn't have auditioning classes then, although they do now. I don't think it is good to teach auditioning, although many would disagree. You should learn how to get past the obstacle of walking into an audition all by yourself because then you retain your own unique way. I have a way of interviewing with someone and a way of preparing for an audition that is different from anyone else's. And the way I am when I walk in the room is about me. I'm not going to do what someone coached me to do or say 'Hello' in a way I was taught, because it always looks like that. Maybe I am awkward sometimes, but so what?

"During the summers I worked at the O'Neill Theatre Center and other places and sometimes, even though Juilliard didn't approve, I worked during the school year. My agent set up an audition with the TV series 'Family Ties.' They were looking for a new girlfriend for Michael J. Fox. The producers were split about hiring me, so they offered me a guest spot. After I did it they offered me an ongoing role on another series, but I couldn't do it because I didn't want to leave school.

"I am glad I did 'Family Ties,' even though it caused me problems at Juilliard. It was a good experience. It's not *Lear*, but it was good just to be in front of the camera. Also, I got the role in the film *Vital Signs* because of it. One of the 'Family Ties' producers mentioned me to a friend who was casting *Vital Signs*. Three days before Juilliard graduation they flew me out to shoot the picture. I graduated from Juilliard, but I didn't participate in the ceremony. It all happened so fast my friends had to move me out of the Y where I had been living.

"Most of my jobs have come about indirectly, similar to *Vital Signs*. It is rare that I audition for a job and get it. It is always a case of my doing an audition and getting some other job because of the audition.

"After *Vital Signs* I had enough money to rent an apartment. But living in New York is impossible to afford. I envy people who did it years ago, because then it was possible to get by. My first apartment was so terrible that I think that if I had to choose between staying there, in Hell's Kitchen, or giving up acting, I would have given up acting. I moved to the Upper West Side, which is better but expensive.

"It is nerve-racking sustaining yourself emotionally and financially as an actress in New York. Also, it is harder for women: we have to buy more clothes and maintain ourselves, and there are fewer roles than for men. I'm a terrible waitress—I get too frazzled—so I never could do that. I love working with kids, so when I needed money I worked as a substitute teacher or I baby-sat. Friends of mine who have done a lot of films can come to New York and do plays in little theatres because they want to play a certain role. For a New York actress that is difficult, not only because of the money but because it takes you away. It is important always to be out there.

"Last summer my agent wanted me to workshop a play up in Saratoga. I didn't want to go, but she strongly advised it. So I went. [The play, *I Hate Hamlet*, was moved to Broadway and Jane received excellent reviews in the press.] The only time I don't feel productive is when I'm not working.

"Sometimes I feel like my life is always on hold. Sometimes I feel like I don't even have a life. What I have is a pile of scripts and messages on my answering machine. Still, I do see myself remaining an actress because in the long run it is what I do better than anything else, so when I'm not doing it I'm not happy."

On Advice to Young Actors

"I would say learn something else and then if you still want to become an actor, go and do it. That is what happened to me. I studied other things but came back to acting.

"If you decide to go into acting without first going to Juilliard or Yale, then I would say don't come straight to New York. Go to Minneapolis, or Seattle, or some other city with a regional theatre, where it is nicer to live and you can get jobs and your Equity card. Then come to New York.

"Someone once told me to be more Zenlike about the whole thing. That was in the beginning, when every audition was a huge big deal and every rejection was worse than the last. What he meant was you are not going to get a lot of parts that you want. And a lot of the time it is the thing that you don't put weight on or give thought to that will end up being very important to you. There is something going on that you don't have control over. That is a relief in a way.

"When I try to hold on and think I can control what happens to me in this business, it turns into a roller-coaster ride. But when I think maybe I'll go to Seattle for a while and cool out, I get a job. If you want the phone to ring, then go take a bath. It is a question of recognizing what you can do and what you have no control over. There is a lot of waiting involved in this business. The important thing for an actor is to move forward."

2

Training

I couldn't see all two hundred actors who sent in their pictures, so the first thing I did was turn all the pictures facedown and look at their résumés. I auditioned only those who went to graduate school. —Bob Moss, director

Training is imperative today for most actors for several reasons. Training provides skills, and skills are what separate the amateurs from the professionals. You may be able to perform an impromptu acting task instinctively with great aplomb, but without the skills of the craft you won't be able to repeat the work.

Training also provides you with the basic tools of an actor: moving and speaking correctly. There was a time when actors could learn by doing. Today, with fewer and fewer theatre companies able to support themselves and films costing millions of dollars, your chances of working in theatre or film as an untrained beginner are almost nil. During Hollywood's Golden Age, studio moguls could and did create stars by molding young, untrained actors into legends. Today the studio star-factory system doesn't exist. School is where young actors get to work and have their talent awakened—but more on that later.

There are also practical reasons for going to school. Agents, casting directors, and directors pay more attention to well-trained actors—especially those trained at serious university drama programs like Juilliard, Yale, North Carolina School of the Arts, and others. When it comes time to audition, the name of a prestigious school such as Juilliard on your résumé will certainly put you ahead of another actor who hasn't been so rigorously trained.

THE PRESENTATIONS

Graduates of prestigious acting programs are often given priority when it comes to auditions. However, there is an even earlier advantage. As a senior at such a school you will participate in an audition process known as "the presentations." The presentations, which usually take place in May, are a kind of mass audition where senior drama majors at certain schools have the chance to be seen by entertainment-business professionals. Universities with good drama programs rent theatres in New York and invite the city's top casting directors, agents, managers, and entertainment executives to come and see their graduates perform. The presentations are a once-in-a-lifetime opportunity to audition for hundreds of people, any one of whom can get your career started.

When we asked agent Stephen Hirsh where he goes to look for new talent he answered: "Like everyone else, we visit the school graduate presentations. This year we went to Yale, Juilliard, Purchase, Boston University, NYU, Carnegie Mellon, A.C.T., Temple, San Diego, Rutgers, North Carolina School of the Arts, and Brandeis University." School presentations aren't the only source of new clients for agents, nor are you guaranteed to find an agent at the presentations, but numerous actors' careers have been launched there.

Until recently, only Juilliard and the Yale School of Drama presented their senior drama majors in this way. Today several schools hold presentations: SUNY-Purchase, Boston University, NYU, Carnegie Mellon, Temple, North Carolina School of the Arts, Brandeis, A.C.T., and others. Students are allowed about six minutes to do a monologue. Agents consider each student and decide whether they want to pursue an actor. Casting directors regard the audition as an introduction to a young actor's work. As casting director Daniel Swee told us: "We see the presentations as a handshake; hopefully we will continue to audition these young actors for the next twenty years." The exposure and experience of auditioning in front of hundreds of people who are in a position to hire or represent you is well worth the anxiety.

The presentations are a wonderful opportunity, but they represent merely the icing on the cake. The real privilege of training is the learning and the opportunity to do good theatre and important plays. Never again in your life will you have the luxury of working in such a concentrated way on excellent theatre unless you become one of the privileged few who are invited to join one of the fine, mostly English, repertory companies.

Theatre has long served as a training ground for beginning actors, but today, with fewer grass-roots theatre companies and the established nonprofit theatres doing fewer plays and using more television and film actors to attract audiences, opportunities have diminished for the novice. School is now the primary source of stage experience for young actors. This is a relatively new trend. A little background helps explain how the lack of theatre opportunity affects budding actors.

■

Bob Moss, now a director and the former artistic director and founder of Playwrights Horizons, one of the most respected not-for-profit theatres in New York City, explains what happened to create this change: "Twenty years ago there was an explosion of theatre companies. First of all there was all this money from the New York State Council on the Arts, the National Endowment, private philanthropy. And at that time all the arts, theatre included, were responding to the political climate in America, so there was a furious burst of activity. Today the NYSCA and the Endowment have limited funds, and private philanthropy has waned. Every year more and more theatre companies bite the dust for economic reasons. So theatre is shrinking. And theatres that have survived are doing much less work. When we started Playwrights we had the beauty of the Showcase Code (an Equity contract allowing actors and some technicians to work for free), which allowed us to spend little money and consequently put up thirty plays a year. Today Playwrights produces five plays a year. All across the country, regional theatres are producing fewer and fewer plays per season to cope with a shrinking economy. The result is, it is harder and harder for actors in this country to work in theatre."

Jane Adams, a graduate of Juilliard, returned to the school two years later to see a production of Romeo and Juliet and learned how profound the theatre experience is for students: "While I was a student, I realized on some level how much is accomplished there. But not until some time had gone by could I see how beautiful it is, what they are trying to accomplish there. I remember William Hurt coming back to see a production of Lear while I was still a student. Afterward, at a party, he said something about how wonderful it was to see that production. He was right—it is great that somewhere they are trying to keep that kind of theatre alive."

Of course, not everyone can attend one of the prestigious conservatories or universities. And some may not want to. There are other routes available in the form of drama schools and individual drama classes. A partial list and more information on these programs is included later in this chapter, as is some guidance in choosing which form of training is right for you—because this is a very personal decision. But one thing is clear—you must have some sort of training; on that everyone agrees. Listen:

Casting director Marion Dougherty: "I read résumés from the bottom up because that is where the training is. To get good training is the most important thing of all."

Actor Jason Alexander: "Study everything. There is nothing I can think of that doesn't make for a better actor. Study acting, voice, dance, mime, masks, movement techniques, Alexander technique. Study psychology, watch people, study languages, learn dialects. Your best Russian accent will come from observing a Russian speaking Russian— because then you'll understand why he has so much trouble wrapping his teeth around his mouth speaking English. Learn how to juggle, do magic tricks, manipulate a puppet, learn how to roller-skate, how to skate-board. Why? Because you might get a show merely because you are the one guy who knows how to sing, dance, and roller-skate. That makes you different than everyone else coming in."

Casting director Alexia Fogel: "Training is vital. Regional theatre work is so important to an actor's career and you will not get that unless you are well trained. Part of it is understanding the language of acting. Directors, especially good ones, are going to use language you need to know in order to communicate. Also, this is the only profession in the world where people believe they can simply say they are actors and be actors. That's not any more true than it is for musicians who must train hours a day before they can play in a concert. Actors need to train too because they need to be disciplined."

Director Bob Moss: "It is tough out there. If you want to participate in this profession, there are certain skills you have to learn, period. You have to learn how to talk and be heard, how to be truthful, how to solve moments, how to rehearse. These are skills and have nothing to do with art. But with the use of these skills you might find your way into something artistic. Great skill can awaken the talent in you. If I have the choice as a director between an untrained actor and a more trained actor, I'm going to take the more trained actor. We speak the same language. I can tell a trained actor that he or she needs an 'as if' here or an 'element' there or an 'emotional memory' here—and he will know what I'm saying. Because we have a common vocabulary I can make suggestions and the trained actor will understand. You don't get art by throwing paint at a canvas. First you learn classical painting techniques; then you have the right to break it apart and throw paint at a canvas because then you know what you are doing. It's the same with acting."

Casting director Juliet Taylor: "I'm a big believer in studying because it allows you to work as much as you possibly can before you really have to sell yourself. Like everything else in our modern society, everyone feels they are something—an actor—just because they *say* they are. But I think you really have to work hard at it before you can call yourself an actor, and keep working all the time."

Casting director Daniel Swee: "All I can say is all good stage actors have trained and trained extensively."

Casting director Kari Strom Bush: "There is so much competition out there, young actors have to be well trained to compete. I go to all the school presentations and you can really see the difference good training makes."

In England actors have always trained for their profession. In America this is a fairly new phenomenon, but a growing one. And while there will always be exceptions to the rules, the smart route today is the training track. It allows you to open yourself up to options; to ready yourself for professional opportunities; to gain the attention and respect of agents and casting directors; to enhance your self-confidence; and, most of all, to earn the right to call yourself an actor. While it's true that no school can teach you how to have that special quality that truly gifted actors seem to possess, you *will* learn how to activate and sustain your raw talent and communicate with other professionals; in the long run that is what counts.

DECIDING WHERE TO STUDY

There are three basic options for the prospective theatre student: a graduate or undergraduate university program like Yale or Juilliard; a long-term drama school like the Neighborhood Playhouse; or individual classes at such places as HB Studio or the Actors Conservatory in New York. Once again, all the professionals interviewed agree the decision is an individual one and must be made after

examining your options and evaluating your circumstances.

Casting director Janet Foster adds: "Deciding when and
where to train is a very personal thing. Some people feel
they need to live first, to get out and travel. Some people
feel they need to go right into a training program after high
school or college, but it is such a personal decision and
depends on where you are in your life."

Training was a part of the plan for all the actors we interviewed. David Lansbury, who co-starred on Broadway
in Wendy Wasserstein's *The Heidi Chronicles,* was
especially purposeful about his training, leaving one program and going to England to study at Central School of
Speech and Drama. The lesson to be learned from David
is that acting training varies greatly, both in philosophy
and technique. The program that is right for you, that
teaches you how to work better and get results, will not
necessarily be right for someone else. Just because a particular school is deemed wonderful by one actor does not
mean it will be so for another. Every actor is unique and
will respond uniquely. Secondly, schools change from
year to year as their staff moves about; a program that is
considered good one year may not be good the next.

There is also the matter of the type of acting technique
taught. In general, there are two overall philosophies: the
internal method is based on the teachings of the Russian
theatre director Stanislavsky and is more concerned with
the emotional aspects of acting; the *external method* is
more concerned with technical skills and more like the
English school of acting. Some actors follow one method
religiously, especially those trained in the so-called
Method as taught by the Actors Studio. Most, however,
create their own method of acting by combining tech-

niques they have learned over the years at various schools and classes.

VOICES

David Lansbury

David Lansbury's experience is particularly noteworthy because he had the foresight to realize things weren't working for him at one school, so he moved on. The important point to David's story is not that there was anything wrong with his original acting school, but that it didn't suit his needs. Rather than give up acting school or just go through the motions, he took responsibility for his training and accomplished his goal.

"The training in New York consisted of a lot of inner work—Stanislavsky, Strasberg, and people from the Actors Studio. There was very little technical training—I realized that from the beginning—but what I didn't realize was how valuable good vocal work could be for me. That is, until I went to England.

"I appreciated the preparation work I learned at my first school. They had fantastic teachers, but I didn't sense any unity of purpose. The teachers met once a year, but I think only to decide which students were going to stay for the next year and which were going to be asked to leave. They cut half the class. Also, we never did any plays, only scene work, and I wanted to do plays. I felt I had to leave. Maybe I was learning something about life, but I wasn't learning about acting. Also, I remembered I used to have fun acting and wasn't any longer. Also at that time I hooked up with an agent who saw me in a presentation we did. He was sending me out to audition for 'tits-and-ass' high school movies. On the one hand I'm studying Stanislavsky; on the other I'm up for all this crap—it was not easy to keep a bit of dignity.

"I knew about the nature of training in England from my dad [producer/director Edgar Lansbury], so I decided to audition for Central. I had auditioned for Juilliard, but I didn't get in.

"The Central audition took place in New York. Most of the English drama schools, like RADA, Webber Douglas, and LAMDA, do auditions in New York. It was a difficult audition and took three days—they kept cutting back every day. My year they only took two Americans out of two hundred who auditioned. I did four monologues, Shakespeare and contemporary. I liked the people who auditioned me, the way they auditioned and the direction they gave me during the audition. I craved some real training. So I went to Central. It is a three-year course; the tuition is cheap and a student visa isn't hard to get.

"We did sonnets and one play a term. A major focus of the teaching was that you 'put on a mask,' you put on the clothes and see how they make you feel. The work we did brought out the talents of the students, and we were encouraged to experiment. It was a relief to be able to make an idiot of myself—to be able to ham it up, make mistakes, and not worry about all that emotional recall stuff. For me it was a much more magical way of working and still is —that kind of transformation is magic, mysterious. All the internal work was covered, but in a more organic, less heavy way. Central claims it has no method—RADA and LAMDA claim they do—but I believe any good technique allows you to find the truth of the text and as much of that truth within you as possible. Anyway, it worked for me, especially the heavy vocal work, because my whole sound function was misguided. It was great doing whole plays—by the end of your three years you do nine full plays.

"Because the profession is taken more seriously in England, I started taking life a little more seriously although I didn't take myself more seriously—I was just a mug who happened to do acting for a living. Somehow that makes it easier for me to live my life and enjoy what I'm doing.

"My English training served me well. I signed with a great English agent who found me at Central, and after I finished school I got a job with the Birmingham Repertory Company. It was a good opportunity. Also, I was able to get my British Equity card because of it. Then I did a television movie for the BBC, a couple more plays—one in London. I had a whole life over there—an apartment, friends, a girlfriend—and I was working constantly, but I knew I wanted to come home eventually, and so I did. I got my agent here in New York through my agent in England."

Alec Phoenix

Alec Phoenix provides an inside glimpse into the audition process and everyday existence at Juilliard. Alec was an economics major at Swarthmore College when he decided to try acting during a summer break. He was hired by a summer-theatre company to work backstage and do some bit parts. By the time Alec got his economics degree he had no interest in the field, so he continued to pursue acting. Alec's good looks caught the attention of an agent to whom he had sent his picture. The agent told him about an Equity job at a dinner theatre. Alec got the job and was offered his Equity card. That year he continued to work as an actor and was hired for three commercials. Although Alec now had his foot in the door, he realized his lack of training could impede his career.

"When you apply to Juilliard they send you a sheet saying you need to prepare two monologues, one classical and one contemporary. They provide suggestions for males and females. The monologues I had chosen were on the list. I had been auditioning a lot that year and was well oiled, so Juilliard was just one more audition, which helped. But what really helped me was the whole process.

"I showed up at nine-thirty in the morning, along with seventy other people. Some of the faculty led us through basic group acting exercises like walking in a circle, changing your movements, and singing as a warm-up. Then I went in and did my two pieces for a panel of three. After that I was asked to do a cold reading, and then to sing in an imaginary situation: I sang 'Happy Birthday' to my dog. Then they posted a callback sheet. Six people out of the 70 were called back. Before the callback I decided to go ice skating in Central Park with a girl I had just met at the audition. That day I just felt on top of the world—I was relaxed. After skating I came back and did my pieces again. This time it was in front of the whole staff and in a bigger studio. Then I was asked to do an exercise: I was in a room, there was a phone, and I was waiting for an important call. It is devastating news. I hang up the phone and sing a song. Through the song I either restrain my emotions or release them. I did the exercise, and something clicked for me—it worked.

"I went off to Rhode Island to do a play and it was there that I got the call to say I was accepted. Then I had second thoughts. It was four years! I was twenty-three and Juilliard is an undergraduate program, you don't get a master's the way you do at Yale. And people in the company said, 'You're working, don't go back to school.' But I decided to go.

"The first year there's a lot of work and little encouragement and it turns some Juilliard students into neurotics. What they do is break you down. And you are constantly confronted with paradoxes: Work on your voice but when you are acting don't think about your voice. They are constantly confusing you but by the end of the first year you are told it is okay to be confused, it will all work itself out. Just trust the program.

"They throw a lot of things at you in class. A little bit of Meisner one day, a little bit of Strasberg emotional memory another day. Ultimately it is up to you to integrate all of this. *Process* is a big word they use: 'What's your process?' And 'Don't be results oriented.' You have to be careful not to be annihilated by it. I went through this whole period of just thinking too much and then I tried not thinking about it at all—don't think, just be. You also do what they call a 'discovery play' in the first year. They give you a classical play to rehearse with a director, but he really won't direct you. You discover how to work for yourself. They discover how naturally you react to classical material and begin to make decisions on how to train you.

"There are cuts after the second year. In our class three people were cut, so we were down to fourteen people. How it happens is you do several rehearsal projects, which is a play put up in a studio without full tech. There are four such projects per year for the first two years. You are critiqued by all your teachers at these projects. They say how they think you are progressing and what they thought of your work in that particular project. By the end of the second year, after your final critique, you go into the office of the head of Juilliard and he says whether you are cut or not.

"You are not supposed to work professionally during your first two years at Juilliard. But during the summer after your second year you can start to do the Shakespeare festivals—Utah, Illinois, Santa Cruz, and Williamstown Theatre Festivals. In fact, they come up to Juilliard to audition students. I think Juilliard is sensing that actors might need to start to work before they graduate, although they still don't encourage it, but they don't condemn it as much, especially if it is a career thing. But it's tough auditioning while you are in school. Juilliard is draining, and I was under-prepared at the auditions I did go on.

"Agents aren't allowed in to see projects until the third year when you start doing 'performance projects.' That is how I got a new agent. At the end of the fourth year for one night you get to present scenes to a select audience of casting directors and agents.

"I heard before I went that Juilliard breaks you down and then builds you up. But I didn't really comprehend that until now. An actor told me, 'Let go of it . . . let go of the grip Juilliard has on you.' That advice is astute. To be inspirational, instruction must be fully integrated into who you are—not hold you captive."

Conservatory or university training is not the solution for every actor. What you gain in being in a secure environment, you lose in audition training. What you gain in getting the attention of agents and casting directors, you lose in being out of circulation. What you gain in participating in a purposeful curriculum, you lose in your ability to customize your training. Overall, however, especially for those just out of high school, you win more than you lose. Unquestionably, as you've heard us and everyone else interviewed say, some sort of training is mandatory.

Jason Alexander experienced both university training and individual-class training; in retrospect, both experiences were beneficial: "When I started BU I was seventeen years old and not ready to leave my parents' home, earn a living, and take classes in New York. But I needed time to be quasi on my own, so a university setting was good for me then. The problem, however, with any multiple-year program is that while you get to choose the school, you don't choose the teachers and the teachers aren't always great, and even if they are great, they don't necessarily 'speak' to you. On the other hand, you can also fumble around the city and land up in classes with teachers who don't know what they are talking about. With private classes, you have to get recommendations from people you trust.

"Two years after I was out of school, I found a teacher, Larry Moss, who literally changed my career. His technique was so disciplined that he taught me dignity and respect for the craft. He made me see that I had skills which I could put together and take my work anywhere I wanted it to go. He made me see that it is not about me, it's about my work, and that's a big difference. He taught acting through song. He was actually teaching you how to do a musical audition, where once the song starts you've got to be ready to go. You can't just wait until you feel the moment. So I learned how to audition in his class."

Ally Sheedy also trained with an assortment of teachers and continues to take class with Harold Guskin in New York at every opportunity. Ally also majored in drama at the University of Southern California: "Through all these classes I picked up some things that work, that I remember and that I use. Other things didn't work for me, but might for someone else. I don't think there is one method of training that works for everybody. It is an individual thing to sort through. But I think you need to. I'm glad I went to all those schools. But if somebody finds one school that is dynamite for them, they should stay with it."

Some actors blossom in a strict classical program, others don't. Some actors flourish with an individual drama teacher; others, a variety of teachers. And some actors still want to train by working in the theatre, a choice that was more available in years past.

James McDaniel took several acting classes around New York but insists his real training began when he started working in the theatre. His on-the-job-training viewpoint is worthwhile because with a subject as personal and critical as your training, you should know all the options: "I can't say training is not a good idea for a lot of people. But for me it just provided me with the sense that 'Yeah, I can do this.' I could be onstage for ten minutes and learn more than I would in a year of acting classes just because it makes a hell of a lot of difference when people are paying to see you. It's all these forces in motion: getting your butt out there, getting reviewed and learning from those professionals that are right next to you. That's how I learned. But I am not saying that it would be good for everyone.

"The one thing I find tremendously lacking in all these young actors who trained in schools is the urge to get a point across. I like to work from a sense of 'I've got to say it.' But what I see a lot of young trained actors do instead of getting a point across is performing well."

James McDaniel is fortunate in that he could be a student of the stage. In actuality, he isn't saying anything drastically different from the other professionals—actors need a solid foundation in theatre training to sustain a career. Unfortunately, today there are few places for young actors to experience on-the-job training. That is why we suggest you have solid training before you enter the open market and throw yourself on its mercy. As in other highly competitive professions, it is generally understood that the applicant with the best qualifications will win out over those who are less qualified.

SCHOOLS

As we have just seen, more and more actors knocking on doors today have had some kind of formal college or university training in drama. Most of the people on the hiring end of the business seem to agree that theatre training at the college level is not only a good idea, but can be a deciding factor.

Besides looking good on your résumé, the background and experience afforded by this kind of training is invaluable. It offers you the opportunity to become involved in all the different facets of theatre or filmmaking. In addition to the training in acting technique and technical skills—speech, voice, movement, dance, analysis of text, scene study, performance experience, and more—there is also the behind-the-scenes experience in designing sets, building lights, making costumes, directing, and producing. College, or a graduate training program, offers a special kind of freedom to test yourself, to learn and explore—a freedom that will be hard to find later in the so-called real world, where the pressures of making a living will be added to the pressures of getting work as an actor.

You will be able to study with good and even excellent teachers. You will have at your disposal the expensive, elaborate facilities that many universities and colleges have in their theatre departments. You will be able to explore different facets of the medium and learn important skills that will give you a greater range and enable you to work within your field, rather than outside it, when you are without an acting job. You will also meet a community of people that may later become an important network for you as well as loyal friends to help you through the hard times. Perhaps you will cohere with a group of fellow actors and form your own independent acting company —like Naked Angels in New York. Most of all, you will earn the right to call yourself an actor.

Choosing the right college or university depends, naturally, on several variables—what colleges you can get into, what you can afford, scholarship opportunities, and location. There are at least a thousand colleges and universities in this country that offer undergraduate programs in drama and many that offer graduate programs.

Here is a select listing of some of the many universities, colleges, and graduate drama schools both here and in London, along with a capsule summary of the nature of the programs offered, academic requirements (if any), admission procedures, and scholarships available. For a comprehensive list we suggest the *Directory of Theatre Training Programs II*, available in drama specialty bookstores or by mail: Theatre Directories, P.O. Box 519, Dorset, VT 05251, or phone (802) 867-2223.

There are generally three different degrees offered at the undergraduate level:

1. Bachelor of Arts degree with a major in drama. This is a broad liberal education with a concentration in theatre.
2. Bachelor of Science degree in theatre education, which will qualify you to teach acting.
3. Bachelor of Fine Arts degree in theatre. This is a preprofessional degree, the purpose of which is to prepare you for a professional career as an actor.

THE JUILLIARD SCHOOL
60 Lincoln Center Plaza
New York, NY 10023-6589
(212) 759-5900

A degree from Juilliard is a prize on anyone's résumé.
Juilliard has a superb reputation for training actors; the
faculty consists of many distinguished performers and
teachers (visiting artists in the past several years have included Patti LuPone, Derek Jacobi, Kelly McGillis, and
Robin Williams); the curriculum emphasizes performance; there is a definite connection between Juilliard
and the professional community, and the senior-year production is attended by key people in the business, agents
and casting directors, and others.

PROGRAM: Juilliard offers two different four-year programs:

1. Bachelor of Fine Arts degree program that, along
   with the drama division courses, also requires completion of twenty-four credits in the Liberal Arts
   department.
2. The Diploma program, which has no liberal arts requirement. The Drama Division courses encompass
   acting, dramatic verse, basic masks, movement,
   voice, speech, singing, comedy techniques, and
   dance. During the first two years students are involved in rehearsal projects, which are laboratory
   exercises for exploring an actor's process and are not
   aimed at performance results. In the third year the
   emphasis shifts from the lab to the theatre. Four or
   five productions are fully mounted. In the fourth
   year, plays are given full-scale production. Four
   plays are produced and mounted two times, the first
   before an invited audience and the second for the

general public and members of the theatrical profession (agents, etc.). Interestingly, the fourth year now
also includes an auditions workshop.

Note: After two years at Juilliard a student's work is
reviewed, and if it is judged to be below that of the
group as a whole, the student is not invited back for
the last two years of the program.

ADMISSION CRITERIA: Students are admitted to Juilliard on
the basis of competitive auditions held at Juilliard and in
selected cities around the country. Applicants are required
to prepare two monologues—one classical and one from
a play written "in the last hundred years," not to exceed
a total of four minutes in length. Juilliard provides a list
of suggested pieces. In addition, applicants may be asked
to sing a cappella. Only twenty new students are admitted
each year out of several thousand applicants. Fewer
graduate.

YALE UNIVERSITY
SCHOOL OF DRAMA/REPERTORY THEATRE
P.O. Box 1903A Yale Station
New Haven, CT 06520

Yale's Department of Drama was established in 1924; the
Yale Repertory Theatre was founded in 1967 to bridge the
gap between training and the practicing professional theatre. "The goal of the Yale School of Drama is to develop
the skills, crafts, and attitudes of its students to prepare
them for careers in the professional theatres, in particular
for the demands of repertory and ensemble productions
in permanent theatre companies such as the Yale Repertory Theatre."

PROGRAM: There are two programs offered at Yale, neither
for the beginning actor. "The program admits talented and

intelligent students who have experience in their field of endeavor."

1. Master of Fine Arts—A three-year program for college graduates.
2. Certificate in Drama—A three-year program for applicants who have been out of high school for at least five years but do not have an undergraduate degree and have been working in the field.

The first year of training focuses on realism, "the foundation for all subsequent instruction." This includes Stanislavskian exercises, scene study, and courses in voice, speech, and movement. The second year (students must be invited to return for the second year) emphasizes the works of Shakespeare and the Jacobeans (i.e. formal verse drama), continued training in voice, speech, and movement, as well as mask work and singing. The emphasis in the third year is on contemporary theatre, and there is opportunity to work with the Yale Repertory Theatre.

ADMISSION CRITERIA: Application, résumé, transcripts, and one professional letter of recommendation. The audition consists of two memorized audition pieces—a classical selection in verse and a modern or contemporary prose piece, not to exceed four minutes total time. Auditions are held in Chicago, San Francisco, and New Haven each year.

CARNEGIE MELLON UNIVERSITY
5000 Forbes Avenue
Pittsburgh, PA 15213

The Department of Drama at Carnegie Mellon is the oldest university-based drama program in the country. Carnegie is a member of the Consortium of Conservatory Theatre

Training programs. Training is classically rooted. There are approximately 200 students in the overall program, which includes acting as well as musical theatre specifically for actors.

PROGRAM: A four-year training program resulting in a BFA in drama is offered. The "Acting Option" includes courses in acting, voice, speech, movement, and dance. The focus is mainly on stagecraft, although it is appropriate for other media. There are no public performances during the first two years. The "Music Theatre Option" includes training in music, dance, and drama.

ADMISSION CRITERIA: You must be a high school graduate and SAT scores are considered, but the audition is the main factor in admission. Carnegie Mellon asks for two contrasting monologues, each two minutes in length, one classical and one contemporary. A recent photo is also required.

SUNY at Purchase
SCHOOL OF THE ARTS
735 Anderson Hill Road
Purchase, NY 10577

SUNY (State University of New York) offers a conservatory method of training. It is one of a select group of programs in the country that is a member of the Consortium of Conservatory Theatre training programs. Approximately 30 students are accepted from 500 hundred applicants each year "to work together for four years as an acting company, gaining the skills and experience to make a smooth transition to the professional arena."

PROGRAM: The Acting Program is a four-year program leading to a BFA degree in acting, with 90 credits required in your major and 30 credits in the College of Letters and Science. At the end of the senior year, students have the chance to audition before an audience of agents, casting directors, and producers. The first two years are devoted to the fundamentals of acting and character and scene work, as well as fencing, mask work, gymnastics, etc. During junior and senior year, students participate in many studio productions, as well as three to four fully mounted productions each year.

ADMISSION CRITERIA: Application, high school records and test scores, letters of recommendation. SUNY asks for a résumé and an 8 × 10 photo. The audition is to consist of two three-minute monologues in contrasting styles. Financial assistance is available.

NEW YORK UNIVERSITY
TISCH SCHOOL OF THE ARTS (TSOA)
Office of Admissions
22 Washington Square North
New York, NY 10011

Tisch School of the Arts was founded in 1965 "to provide a matrix for both the formal training and education and the continued artistic growth of young artists and scholars, as well as to assist in improving and reshaping the standards of performance, repertoire, creativity and scholarship in New York City and the nation as a whole." The Institute of Performing Arts has both a graduate acting program and an undergraduate program.

PROGRAM:

1. The Department of Drama at TSOA offers a four-year BFA program for undergraduates that combines professional theatre training in one of a selected

group of five New York acting schools (listed below) with liberal arts study. Three days a week are devoted to training in a professional conservatory. This variety of training options is unique to TSOA. A comprehensive curriculum in dramatic literature is also part of the program. For the third year there are two programs of study offered in London or Paris. Also, third- and fourth-year students can apprentice with a theatre company in lieu of performing the regular studio requirement. Approximately 350 students are selected each year.

ADMISSION CRITERIA: High school records and SAT scores, as well as an audition-interview consisting of two three-minute monologues. Formal audition/interviews are held in February and March in various cities across the country. Photograph required. Regarding grades, a minimum high school average of C+ and a combined SAT score of 1000 or more is required. Financial aid is available.

AFFILIATED TSOA STUDIOS:

The Stella Adler Conservatory of Acting

The Circle in the Square Theatre School

The Lee Strasberg Theatre Institute

The Experimental Theatre Wing

The Playwrights Horizons Theatre School

(For more information about their individual programs, see Commercial Acting Schools, listed below, pp. 60–66.)

2. MFA Graduate Acting Program:

This is a professional, intensive, three-year training program designed "to provide exceptionally talented acting students with the fullest and widest range of skills that can be applied with high standards of imagination and intelligence to the realities of a working career." The goal of the program is "to liberate the acting instrument in terms of voice, body, and inner technique for the creation of character in a wide range of the world's repertory." Competition for admission to this program, which admits only about twenty students per year, is intense.

FIRST YEAR: Emphasis is placed on "freeing" the acting instrument through acting, voice, and movement classes.

SECOND YEAR: The student progresses from scene work to full performance. Character development, action, language, and analysis are emphasized.

THIRD YEAR: Students focus on advance workshops and performance projects, which are open to members of the profession as well as the university community. In addition, there is an opportunity to prepare for professional auditioning.

ADMISSION CRITERIA: Auditions are required, consisting of two two-minute one-person scenes that reveal the range of the actor's talent. Photograph and résumé are also required. Auditions are held in New York and several other major cities across the country in January and March.

NORTH CAROLINA SCHOOL OF THE ARTS
THE UNIVERSITY OF NORTH CAROLINA
200 Waughton Street, P.O. Box 12189
Winston-Salem, NC 27117-2189

The North Carolina School of the Arts, founded in 1963, is a "cluster of conservatories . . . a complex institution with a single, bold mission: to train talented young men and women for professional careers in dance, music, drama, and theatrical design and production." The environment of the school is like that of an artistic colony. The School of Drama responds to a "definite need in the profession for actors to be versatile and technically well-equipped, as well as creatively inspired," and its training program is grounded in an affirmation of classical values.

PROGRAM: Two different four-year programs are offered:

1. The undergraduate BFA degree program combines intensive training in drama with a full academic program.
2. The Arts Diploma program concentrates solely on training in drama.

ADMISSION CRITERIA: Admission is by audition and interview. High school graduation is required for the Arts Diploma program. For the BFA degree program, minimum academic requirements are combined SAT scores of 800 and a high school diploma. Financial aid is available.

AUDITIONS: National auditions, conducted in association with the Consortium of Conservatory Theatre training programs, are held in New York, Chicago, L.A., San Francisco, Houston, and Miami. (The Consortium also includes Boston University, Carnegie Mellon University, and the State University of New York at Purchase. It is an alliance of professional-theatre-training institutions formed to prepare gifted actors for professional careers in theatre, joined together in order to assert standards for training, encourage public recognition, and influence policy in support of the development of theatre artists.)

AUDITION REQUIREMENTS: Two contrasting monologues, two minutes each. The student may also be asked to sing. The School of Drama also offers a summer session for high school and college-level students, which is a way to explore a budding interest in actor training.

BOSTON UNIVERSITY
SCHOOL OF THEATRE ARTS
Office of Admissions
121 Bay State Road
Boston, MA 02215

The Boston University School for the Arts encompasses three separate schools, one of which is the School of Theatre Arts, offering undergraduate and graduate conservatory training programs supplemented with courses in the liberal arts. The training is classical stage training especially geared to prepare a student for work in regional theatre. There are approximately 170 undergraduates and 30 graduate students in the school.

PROGRAM: The undergraduate study program in acting includes stagecraft, rehearsal, and performance as well as a related range of liberal arts requirements. The school puts on five complete productions each year in addition to thirty-five to forty faculty-supervised and -coached projects.

ADMISSION CRITERIA: Application, transcripts, test scores, letter of recommendation. An audition is also required. Early application is suggested, to allow for audition scheduling. Financial aid is available.

MASON GROSS SCHOOL OF THE ARTS
RUTGERS, THE STATE UNIVERSITY OF NEW JERSEY
Levin Theatre, Douglass Campus
New Brunswick, NJ 08903

MGSA was established at Rutgers in 1976. The BFA program is designed for students who plan to work professionally in the field of theatre arts. The school admits approximately 440 students into the overall program. Professional conservatory training is offered in acting, theatrical design, and production management. The acting program "works on the principle that acting is a creative art and that true excellence in its practice may only be attained through total mastery of technical craft." William Esper, who has taught at his own studio in New York for many years, is head of the acting program.

PROGRAM: The BFA program in acting consists of 18 to 21 hours a week devoted to acting, speech, and movement classes. The remainder is devoted to liberal arts courses.

ADMISSION CRITERIA: Applicants undergo general undergraduate admissions procedures as well as an audition/interview, the audition consisting of two one-minute memorized monologues, one contemporary and one classical.

Of course, this is only a partial listing of some of the more prestigious schools that have the respect of the professional community and offer a young actor excellent training, a full range of experience, and preparation for the road ahead. A degree from any of these schools will get you well on your way with training that will enable you to cope with and be creative in a wide variety of professional situations.

COMMERCIAL ACTING SCHOOLS

Nearly every actor has spent time in and money on acting school, in classes, in a workshop. And for the most obvious reason: most actors are out of work much of the time and thus have a real need for classes of one form or another —simply so they can work on their craft. "I think one of the most important things about training is doing those things which make you feel like an actor, because so much time is spent doing things that don't necessarily have very much to do with acting," is the comment of Naomi Thornton, a professional actor as well as a teacher of acting.

"An artist can paint, a pianist can play, a writer can write, and the actor has the glass, the mirror, and can stand in front of it putting different hats on and reciting to herself. It's like a big love affair. But it's not enough. You have got to have the audience and the feedback." That's how one actress explains the need for actors to find a school, a theatre group, or a workshop. Acting school can be a base, an entrée, a good point of contact, and a place to be involved with fellow actors who are doing what you are doing, at all the different stages of the process. There are friends to be made and information to be gathered, networking to be done and leads to follow up. Although you'll be working alongside people you will perhaps be competing with sooner or later, for now you are all in the same boat. And you are part of a community.

There is a wide selection of commercial schools to choose from, and the best advice we heard over and over again when it comes to making a choice was "AUDIT CLASSES!"

"I audited lots of classes and I ditched a lot of studios because I was very particular. You have to go to classes and find out how you want to be taught, and then, if you want to go into more major training, do that," commented one young New York actor.

Auditing is permitted in many of the schools and is a very intelligent way to decide whether or not a particular class or teacher or method suits your needs. The level of teaching can swing from superb to a waste of money, so it is wise to get a taste of the teacher and a feel for the class before committing yourself financially. Most com-

mercial acting schools will accept you after a brief interview and, of course, a quick credit check. Classes can range
from quite reasonable to quite expensive (although price
is not necessarily indicative of quality). Also, acting
schools attract people who are not necessarily particularly
serious about the profession, and many students are there
only to "see what it's like," responding to the built-in
appeals of a social life, attention, fun, and the therapeutic
effects of self-expression.

There are many commercial acting schools in cities
throughout the country. We are going to list several of the
best-known schools in New York City, Chicago, and Los
Angeles. An interesting book to read on the subject of
acting teachers is *The New Generation of Acting Teachers*
by Evan Meckler (Viking).

THE STELLA ADLER CONSERVATORY OF ACTING
130 West 56th Street
New York, NY 10019

One of the top theatrical training institutes for forty years,
this school was founded by Stella Adler, the only American to study privately with Konstantin Stanislavsky. It
offers courses for full-time day students or evening students, professional workshops, and the college-credit program through NYU's Tisch School of the Arts.

PROGRAMS:

1. Two-year program: The first year is devoted to Stella
   Adler's principles of the technique of acting, including movement, voice, scene study, character,
   and text. In the second year, full-length projects are

worked on during the spring semester, to be performed at the end of the school year.

ADMISSION CRITERIA: An interview is the only requirement for most classes; auditions are required for more advanced classes.

2. NYU TSOA degree program: Encompasses acting technique, Shakespeare, styles, text, voice, and movement, along with the NYU liberal arts curriculum. In the fourth year, a full production is presented by the students in the NYU Tisch School of the Arts Theatre.

THE CIRCLE IN THE SQUARE THEATRE SCHOOL
1633 Broadway, on 50th Street
New York, NY 10019

Accredited by the National Association of Schools of Theatre, this school was founded in 1961 to train actors for the professional theatre. "Our intention is that actors trained at the Circle in the Square will have the range and ability to perform all styles and forms of theatre, and that their talents can be drawn upon to support the outstanding tradition of theatre for which the Circle in the Square is renowned." Both the traditional and the experimental are encompassed. Because of the school's connection to the Circle in the Square theatre, students have the chance to observe rehearsals of main-stage productions as well as meet in discussion groups with the cast and the directors.

PROGRAMS:

1. There is a Professional Workshop offered, which is a two-year conservatory program of advanced actor training. In the first year the focus is on technical

skills and an understanding of the actor's working process. The second year (thirty-six students are admitted to the first year; continuation to the second year is by invitation) concentrates on style, character, performance, and more difficult material. Graduating students are presented in a professional scene night that is attended by people in the industry, thus giving the student a chance to be seen and to make important contacts in the business.

ADMISSION CRITERIA: Application, audition, interview, and review. The audition consists of two contrasting monologues.

2. TSOA at Circle in the Square:
This is a four-year course for TSOA students. Students spend three days in studio acting classes at Circle in the Square and two days in academic courses at NYU. The first two years concentrate on acting technique, scene study, speech and voice, singing interpretation, and jazz dance and movement. In the third year, while continuing master classes, there is an emphasis on class workshop projects. Fourth-year students perform in main-stage productions.

ADMISSION CRITERIA: Application, audition, interview, and review. The audition consists of two contrasting monologues, contemporary and classical, no more than five minutes total length.

THE LEE STRASBERG THEATRE INSTITUTE
115 East 15th Street
New York, NY 10003
(branches in Los Angeles and London)

"The work for the actor lies in two areas: the ability to create reality and the ability to express that reality. It is possible for an actor to experience but be unable to express himself without proper training. Relaxation and concentration, spontaneity and awareness lead to a balancing of these opposites." The program offered was created by Lee Strasberg and the technique is known as the "Method" or "Method acting." The teachers at the institute school have thorough knowledge of Strasberg's work.

PROGRAMS:

1. Introductory programs: Twelve-week programs, offered four times a year, which consist of two four-hour basic acting classes per week. The basic acting class is devoted at first to Method work exercises, such as sense memory exercises. Later, students engage in scene study and monologue work.
2. Full-time program: Twenty-two hours of classes per week for thirty-six weeks, including basic acting classes, singing or speech class, a dance or movement class, and various electives.
3. Part-time program: Two basic acting classes per week for forty-eight weeks.

ADMISSION CRITERIA: Admission is by interview only. A program of study is designed to meet an actor's individual needs, once he or she is accepted into the school.

THE EXPERIMENTAL THEATRE WING
721 Broadway
New York, NY 10003

The Experimental Theatre Wing (or ETW) was founded in 1976 as a workshop milieu in which experimental theatre companies and artists could exchange ideas and techniques. The program is based on the work of Jerzy Grotowski and Stanislavsky as well as movement and dance.

ETW is "committed to producing performers who can create their own material."

ETW offers a three-year curriculum, plus a fourth year with several options, including study in the Experimental Theatre Wing–in–Paris program.

THE PLAYWRIGHTS HORIZONS THEATRE SCHOOL
412 West 42nd Street
New York, NY 10036

Playwrights Horizons Theatre School, part of Playwrights Horizons, one of New York's most successful nonprofit theatres, was founded as a studio for the New York University Tisch School of the Arts undergraduate drama department. It also offers a Professional Training Program. The school serves 400 students annually.

PROGRAMS:

1. Two-year program: Four courses each semester, plus a one-act project for Junefest. During summer, students participate in an intensive ten-week workshop at the Hangar Theatre in Ithaca, New York. Second year: Students prepare a full-length project for Junefest, plus take two supporting classes. A final project is presented in September. The goal of the full-time program is "to develop and prepare students for the professional world and also offer its graduates an artistic home."

2. TSOA program at Playwrights Horizons: This program is geared for students interested in studying theatre from "a broader base." It combines acting training with courses in design, directing, stage management, and producing.

HB STUDIO
120 Bank Street
New York, NY 10014

This highly esteemed school was founded by Herbert Berghof in 1945 for the purpose of establishing a theatre of experimentation based on classic tradition. "Conceived as a work place, an artist's home, it offers an outlet for practice and growth for theatre professionals and the opportunity for the young to establish roots in their intended craft." Uta Hagen, one of the country's best acting teachers, and Berghof's wife, has taught there since 1947. She is the author of *A Challenge for the Actor* (Scribners), which we recommend reading. Former HB students include Ron Silver, Judd Hirsch, Maureen Stapleton, and Jason Robards. There are approximately 2000 students in the school. HB offers a full-time program that consists of at least six classes per week. Required are classes in technique, scene study, speech, and movement, with the other two classes being electives.

No audition or interview is required unless indicated for certain more advanced classes.

ENSEMBLE STUDIO THEATRE INSTITUTE
FOR PROFESSIONAL TRAINING
549 West 52nd Street
New York, NY 10019

Founded in 1978, this is the teaching branch of the Ensemble Studio Theatre, one of the country's leading developmental theatres.

PROGRAMS: They offer a two-year full-time interdisciplinary program with an emphasis on acting, directing, or playwriting. The program is designed for "highly motivated individuals wishing to undertake an intensive training program in preparation for a career in the professional theatre." Classes are chosen with the guidance of the program director to complement each other. Eight classes are taken per year, spread out over three terms. Part-time classes are also available.

ADMISSION CRITERIA: An interview with the teacher is required; an audition is required for advanced classes.

NEIGHBORHOOD PLAYHOUSE SCHOOL OF THE THEATRE
340 East 54th Street
New York, NY 10022

Founded in 1928 with an enrollment of nine students, the Neighborhood Playhouse has continued to be one of the leading theatrical training schools to offer professional training for "the serious-minded theatre student." Some famous-name former students include Gregory Peck, Tony Randall, Eli Wallach, Robert Duvall, Dabney Coleman, Diane Keaton, Mary Steenburgen, Amanda Plummer—and many more. Sanford Meisner, a teacher there since 1935, developed a now-famous training technique (taught by many others as well) known as the "Meisner Technique." We suggest reading *Sanford Meisner on Acting* (Random House) for more information about the training process offered at the Neighborhood Playhouse.

PROGRAMS:

1. Two-year program: The curriculum consists of full-day training, five days a week, in acting, dance, speech, voice, and other related theatre arts, such as movement and fencing. Admission to the second year of training is based on approval of the student's work in the first year. At the end of the second year the students have an opportunity to show their work

to an invited audience of professionals in the business, including directors, producers, and agents. While a student is studying at the Neighborhood Playhouse, he or she is not permitted to work professionally.

2. Summer program: The Neighborhood Playhouse has a six-week summer session offering a condensed curriculum that includes courses in acting technique, speech, and movement related to acting. Admission to the program is through an application and interview and is limited to high-school graduates.

ADMISSION CRITERIA: Personal interview, references, and "in certain cases an audition may be required." Students must have a high-school diploma. No financial aid is available.

THE ACTORS STUDIO
432 West 44th Street
New York, NY 10036

The Actors Studio is a nonprofit organization dedicated to the development of actors, playwrights, and directors. In existence for more than forty years, "it was formed to provide a place where young and old professional actors could work together between jobs, or during long runs to continue to develop their craft and to experiment with new forms in creative theatre work." It was founded in 1947 by Elia Kazan, Cheryl Crawford, and Robert Lewis and currently has 800 members. Lee Strasberg was artistic director until his death in 1982. Currently Frank Corsaro directs. The Actors Studio gained its fame and reputation in large part for nurturing the talents of actors like Marlon Brando, Marilyn Monroe, and Al Pacino. Its cachet is somewhat diminished today although alumni continue to participate in activities as well as nurture new members.

MEMBERSHIP: The Actors Studio is not a drama school. Only professional actors over the age of eighteen are eligible to audition for membership, and getting accepted is difficult. The audition consists of a five-minute monologue or scene. There are branches of the Actors Studio in New York and Los Angeles, and once admitted as a member an actor has free use of the studio's facilities. "The actor now has a home in which to work."

THE NEW ACTORS WORKSHOP
259 West 30th Street
New York, NY 10001

The New Actors Workshop, founded in 1988 by Mike Nichols, George Morrison, and Paul Sills, offers a two-year professional actor training program for college students. Thirty-two students are admitted to the first-year class. The program "is designed as a deeply involving transformational journey, challenging the student intellectually, emotionally, physically and facilitating the development of a generative, joyful relation to acting." It offers extensive work with Viola Spolin's improvisational theatre training along with a thorough grounding in Stanislavsky-based "method" technique.

PROGRAM: The program includes classes in acting technique, scene study, improvisation, voice, bodywork, and, in the second year, speech. Classes meet five days a week for a minimum of twenty-four hours a week. Additional time is devoted to preparation. At the end of the second year the students perform for a professional audience of agents, directors, and casting personnel.

ADMISSION CRITERIA: College graduates are preferred. Admission is by application as well as by audition and interview, which are held in Chicago and New York in January. The audition consists of two contrasting speeches chosen from contemporary American drama, no longer than six minutes total. Videotaped auditions are accepted. Admission to the second year is by invitation only.

ACT (AMERICAN CONSERVATORY THEATRE)
450 Geary Street
San Francisco, CA 94102

ACT was founded in 1965 by William Ball as both a theatre and a conservatory that function together. Many of the members of the company teach the students in the conservatory, and many of the students go on to become members of the company. It is the only independent theatre in the country that is fully accredited to grant an MFA to its qualifying students.

PROGRAMS: There are four programs offered by the conservatory.

1. Advanced Training Program: This is a two-year course of actor training at the graduate level for people who have chosen the theatre as a profession. An MFA degree in acting may be awarded to students who hold a B.A. from an accredited college and who complete the two-year program with distinction. (A Professional Theatre Internship, a third year of training, is available by invitation.) The ATP curriculum, which is entirely compulsory, includes training in vocal production; speech; ballet and contemporary dance; stage movement; yoga; combat; Alexander technique; principles of verse; text analysis; acting, which ranges from classwork to rehearsal and performance; and special subjects such as singing and makeup.

ADMISSION CRITERIA: Applicants must be high school graduates and at least twenty years old. Enrollment is by audition and interview only. The audition consists of one selection from Shakespeare and one from a contemporary play, totaling less than five minutes. Auditions are held in San Francisco, New York, Chicago, and Los Angeles between February and April.

2. Summer Training Congress: This is a ten-week program of intensive professional training in the same subjects as those provided in the ATP program.

ADMISSION CRITERIA: Application and a diagnostic audition for placement purposes consisting of two monologues, one classical and one contemporary, totaling five minutes.

3. The Academy: This is a program for students eighteen years and older. There are four ten-week sessions each year, with classes meeting once a week for three hours in the evening or on Saturday. The Academy Certificate Program is an advanced academy program requiring students to complete ten required courses within four consecutive sessions.

ADMISSION CRITERIA: Audition and interview.

**SOUTH COAST REPERTORY/
PROFESSIONAL CONSERVATORY
655 Town Center Drive
P.O. Box 2197
Costa Mesa, CA 92628**

This is a summer program offered by Tony Award–winning South Coast Repertory. It is an eight-week intensive acting program geared to preparing actors for the challenges of the real world of acting.

PROGRAM: Classes are held in acting, with an emphasis on audition skills, audition techniques, script analysis, voice, Shakespeare, and improvisation. Each student is given a personal evaluation at the end of the eight-week course. The students also give a performance before an invited audience of theatre and industry professionals.

ADMISSION CRITERIA: Students must be at least eighteen years old and submit an application. Auditions are held each March. Videotaped auditions are accepted for students living outside Southern California.

South Coast Repertory also has an Adult Conservatory program, offering evening courses for adults. The coursework consists of four nine-week sessions that provide the basics of acting in addition to more intensive training in specific techniques—for example, acting for the camera, auditions and monologues, and acting the classics.

ADMISSION CRITERIA: Admission is by application.

SCHOOLS IN LONDON
Some of the most distinguished drama schools are located in Britain. England has a long tradition of professional theatre. After all, it is the source of the great playwright Shakespeare. Imports from London theatre now dominate Broadway; unfortunately, American plays don't seem to fare as well in London, even when they are very successful on Broadway. The English are traditionally much more serious about the profession of acting and not as commercially, mass market–minded about what they do. At the same time there is the weight of historical tradition, which perhaps limits the artistic license and avant garde creativity one frequently finds in the United States.

It is important to remember that the policy in Britain is to maintain employment for British artists, so work for American actors is restricted. This policy may seem unfair, but a similar policy is in effect here.

The following drama schools in London have distinguished reputations and seem to get high marks from American actors as well as those on the other side of the desk, i.e., casting directors, directors, agents, and producers.

ROYAL ACADEMY OF DRAMATIC ART
62–64 Gower Street
London WC1E 6ED
England

Founded in 1904 by Sir Herbert Beerbohm Tree, the Royal Academy of Dramatic Art has provided a continuous and comprehensive training program for the professional theatre ever since.

The Acting Course is a three-year program with terms beginning in January, May, and September. It is described as an "arduous course" with long working days followed by individual classes and public performances in the evening.

The Acting Course is divided into two parts: intensive work on individual skills (voice, movement, physical skills); and application of those skills to group projects and productions for public performance. The basis of group work is the acting class, and teaching is based on Stanislavsky. There is also a term devoted to technical-craft training.

ADMISSION CRITERIA: Only 30 students are admitted each year. There are no specific academic requirements, although "a good education is advantageous."

AUDITION AND INTERVIEW: The audition consists of two pieces of the applicant's own choosing, no more than three minutes each. One piece must be a monologue from any play by Shakespeare or another Elizabethan/Jacobean playwright, and the other a monologue from a play by another author and in "clear contrast to the first piece." Auditions are held in New York every year.

NOTE: Students at RADA are not allowed to have jobs while studying because the workday is long and intense; thus you must be able to afford to live in London and pay the tuition without working. (Of course, if you are not a citizen, you are not allowed to work, anyway . . .) RADA has another rule that students are not allowed to accept any professional work or sign with an agent prior to completing the course at RADA. The Academy diploma is awarded upon successful completion of the program.

CENTRAL SCHOOL OF SPEECH AND DRAMA
Embassy Theatre
Eton Avenue
London NW3 3HY
England

Central School was founded in 1906 by Elsie Fogerty, who, with Sir Frank Benson, set out to devise a new form of training in speech and drama for young actors. Calling the school "central" was intended to indicate a new, more conservative form of training characterized by a definite body of principles rather than an assortment of different methods and theories.

PROGRAM: The Diploma in Acting is a three-year full-time course that "sets out to prepare students for the widest possible range of work in every branch of the theatre and related media." The development of the student's imagination is at the core of the work. The emphasis is on the idea that acting, movement, and voice are all aspects of one activity and not separate subjects. Singing, dancing, and musical theatre are important elements in the training. The Diploma in Acting offers students either or both of two "pathways"—the theatre pathway or the musical-theatre pathway. In the second year the training of students in musical theatre emphasizes singing and dancing. The students in the theatre pathway get an opportunity to work in video and radio.

ADMISSION CRITERIA: None. Age range seventeen to twenty-five years old.

Auditions are held in New York in the spring. No grants are offered for foreign students. There are no residential accommodations.

THE LONDON ACADEMY OF MUSIC AND DRAMATIC ART
Tower House
226 Cromwell Road
London SW5 0SR
England

Founded in 1861, LAMDA is an independent drama school that describes itself as "progressive and innovative." Students perform in experimental productions in its MacOwan Theatre in the third year. The three-year acting course is dedicated to giving its acting students full-time training to equip them for the highly competitive acting professions.

The work is divided into two areas: organic training of the body and development of the actor's understanding of the process of acting. The last year is devoted to rehearsal and performance and includes practical advice and audition practice.

ADMISSION CRITERIA: Age eighteen to twenty-six. No academic qualifications necessary.

Auditions are held in London, New York, Los Angeles, Toronto, and Vancouver and consist of two contrasting pieces, three minutes each, one from Shakespeare and one from a twentieth-century playwright.

NOTE: Students from abroad are expected to take only the first two years of the three-year course.

In addition, LAMDA offers a one-year postgraduate acting course for overseas students (Fullbright Overseas Course), which is very popular. The course concentrates on performing English classics and includes classes in voice, movement, stage combat, period movement, Alexander technique, mask and tap, and more.

After completion of the third term, students participate in audition practice. Auditions for this one-year course are held in New York, L.A., Toronto, Vancouver, and London in April annually. The audition consists of two contrasting pieces, three minutes each, one from Shakespeare and the other from a Restoration or eighteenth-century English writer or from a play by George Bernard Shaw, Oscar Wilde, Edward Albee, or Tennessee Williams.

WEBBER DOUGLAS ACADEMY OF DRAMATIC ART
30 Clareville Street
London SW7 5AP
England

Founded in 1906 as an opera school in Paris, Webber Douglas Academy moved to London in 1926 and has been a drama school since 1945. Angela Lansbury, Stewart Granger, and Terence Stamp are three of its many notable former students.

Webber Douglas offers three different diploma courses:

a three-year full-time course, a two-year full-time course, and a postgraduate one-year course.

"The core of the course remains the development of skills primarily to enable the student actor to cope with the demands of the classical stage. Once this is achieved, the needs of the modern theatre, films, TV, and radio can be satisfied by building on these foundations."

AUDITION: One Shakespeare piece and one modern piece, three minutes each.

OTHER PLACES TO TRAIN

Private Coaches
Using a private coach will be more expensive, but the advantage to a private coach is the concentrated attention you will get. Seek recommendations and ask questions of current and former students. Know why you want to use a coach; have a specific goal in mind. Perhaps you need to work on monologues, or improve your auditioning skills, or practice cold readings.

Auditioning Classes
Some casting directors offer classes that purport to teach you how to audition. The rather seductive selling point of these classes is that you will be learning how to "cold read" or audition in front of real, live casting directors (the inference being that they may go on to actually cast you in something). However, buyer beware. The legitimacy of these classes is a real issue among the better casting directors, and the Casting Society of America, the professional association of casting directors, is of the opinion that many of these kinds of classes are unethical. Of course, there are some very good classes in auditioning available; these are usually offered by a reputable studio

or acting school and good casting directors. Check credentials. If the casting director works for a major network, theatre, or film studio, he or she will probably have something to teach you. If the credentials are questionable or obscure, we suggest caution.

Additionally, the new trend at colleges and drama schools is to bring in casting directors for guest seminars on the art of auditioning. This might be a good question to ask of a casting director offering classes in auditioning: Have you ever taught a seminar at a good drama school or college?

Workshops

An alternative to paying for classes, which actors find themselves unable to do when times are lean, is to form your own independent group or workshop, as this actor has done: "I've cut back on classes, and I am doing what I think a lot of actors can get into, because after a certain amount of training you just have to keep working on your craft. I do two workshops with friends. In one workshop we do singing auditions for each other. We all studied with the same singing teacher, and we work on our individual programs. In the other group, we have all had college training and we do scene classes. By now we all have a good idea of what parts we are right for and so it's a very practical situation which gives us the structure that we need to work."

Other Kinds of Classes

While most commercial acting schools offer dance classes and movement classes, you can find classes in exercise, dance, t'ai chi, yoga, aerobics, etc., almost anywhere. These classes can be very cheap and very good. Similarly, classes in voice and singing for the actor are offered in most acting schools, and you can also get private instruction. Private classes will be more expensive, but if you feel you would benefit from them, it is sensible to ask around and get a recommendation from an acting teacher or fellow student.

Wrap-up

Naomi Thornton, acting teacher, sums up why she feels professional study is invaluable: "I think one of the most interesting things about studying acting is that you then have the tools not just to be part of the world, but to shape the world, and that's a hard concept for actors to grasp. There is something really quite medieval about acting where actors stand in line for jobs and wait to be given something. There is very little suggestion that they can do anything about their lives themselves as artists. The tradition is to wait, and we have to change that."

The product of all your hard work, preparation, and training is you. No one else can turn you into a good actor, no matter how inspiring he or she might be. And if you are serious and ambitious and realistic (also brave and daring), you will want to feel prepared and be prepared—ready for anything when you are called on to perform. Training will help a lot. Many of the schools mentioned in this section talk about "preparing the student for a life in the professional theatre." But you have to put yourself out there, and the best way to get out there is to be ready. Remember that in the beginning you will be your own product, advertising agency, and salesman, and no one but you can get the attention of your audience, inspire it, fascinate it, surprise it, and move it.

3

Where the Work Is

There is this continual buzz in New York that's telling
everybody to move to L.A. because that is where the
work is. It is almost like you have to go there and do a
series or film just so you can come back here to do a
play.
                                        —Jane Adams, actress

THEATRE

Fifteen years ago, when the first edition of this book was
written, this chapter began: "If this book were being written fifteen years ago, it would be realistic to put Broadway
at the head of the list as a place where actors could look
for work and start their careers. Today, however, times
have changed."

Yet another fifteen years brings more frightful news for
actors dreaming of coming to New York to work. Today
the above statement could apply to New York theatre in
general. Yes, New York is still the theatre capital of the
United States, but New York is not the best place for un-

developed actors to start their careers. There are many reasons for this.

Today the Broadway stage is filled with Hollywood movie stars and experienced acting talent from all over the world. Even off-Broadway theatres have their choice of seasoned talent—from the world of television, film, and even London. Off-off-Broadway still affords some opportunities for young talent, but fewer shows are being produced. The competition for work in New York theatre is tougher than ever; so are living conditions.

The good news is that throughout the United States regional theatres abound and, in some cases, are thriving. In cities such as Seattle, Chicago, Costa Mesa, Pittsburgh, and Minneapolis, theatre companies are producing new American plays as well as classics. In fact, many of the plays that find their way to New York originate in what is referred to as "regional theatre." This is the arena where many of today's young actors test the waters. Don't expect open arms, but the terrain is somewhat friendlier than New York.

Some background on theatre activity throughout the country will give you a grasp on your options. But first a little history. Until the 1930s, American theatre was a commercial enterprise. That is, producers mounted plays to sell tickets and make a profit. In 1931, the Group Theatre was formed by Cheryl Crawford, Lee Strasberg, and Harold Clurman in an attempt to break away from commercialism. The Group's aim was to broaden the art and content of the American theatre and to encourage new playwrights to write about serious, relevant issues. The Group Theatre lasted only ten years, but it was the precursor of the noncommercial theatre movement, an activity that changed the face of American theatre forever.

Also known as not-for-profit theatre, noncommercial theatre began to take shape in the late 1950s. Several events led to its creation: rising costs; a tax-reform act in which individuals were allowed a tax deduction for donations to a cultural institution; the formation, in 1965, of the National Endowment for the Arts, which used public monies to support the arts; and, lastly, a collective outburst of creative activity in the 1960s and 1970s.

With money and creative energy pouring in, theatre expanded everywhere, not only in New York but across the country. The euphoria was short-lived. By the 1980s donations were down and, most critically, government funding was slashed to a bare minimum. Only the healthiest noncommercial theatres survived, and many of those did so by producing successful new plays that could be "moved" to a commercial theatre and thereby earn a profit.

Regardless of its hardships, noncommercial theatre survives and is the backbone of theatre in this country. In order to understand where the work is in theatre today, it might be helpful to divide the subject in two: the commercial and not-for-profit arenas.

Commercial theatre headquarters are in New York, but there is commercial theatre activity elsewhere in the country. Commercial theatre is produced by producers and theatre owners who raise money from various backers, known as angels. Commercial theatre can only be performed in theatres deemed commercial houses by the various entertainment unions. The unions prescribe the rules, regulations, and salary requirements for actors and behind-the-scenes personnel via various contracts. There are contracts for Broadway theatres, off-off-Broadway, dinner theatre, summer stock, children's theatre, bus-and-truck companies, etc. Designation of theatre type is based on the number of seats in the house, the location of the theatre, the budget, and such variables as whether the show was written for children, or that dinner will be served during the performance. An actor performing in a commercial theatre generally must be a member of Equity, the actors' theatrical union.

In most instances a major distinction between commercial and not-for-profit is that commercial producers work on a show-to-show basis. Each production is treated as a separate entity. A successful commercial producer might have more than one show running at the same time, but for each production a new theatre must be found, as well as a new audience. And most importantly to you, for each commercial production there is a new director and casting director to audition for. Every now and then a commercial producer or major-league actor tries to create a commercial theatre company that operates much like a not-for-profit company—except that they intend to make a profit. Thus far, none of these enterprises has endured.

Not-for-profit theatre is an umbrella term for all kinds of theatrical activity: regional theatre, some off Broadway, most off-off-Broadway, and cultural institutions. Most not-for-profit theatre is produced by a theatre company that consists of a permanent facility and regular staff, headed by an artistic director and almost always including an on-staff casting director. Some not-for-profit theatre companies invite guest directors to direct a particular play, while others have the same director for all their productions. Not-for-profit theatre depends on grants and donations, as well as subscriptions, individual ticket sales, and profits from any of their productions that might be moved to a commercial theatre. A prime example is *A Chorus Line*, a play that for years provided money for the not-for-profit New York Shakespeare Festival. Money earned by not-for-profit theatre companies is used to pay its staff, production people, and actors. Surplus money is put back into the theatre. The majority of not-for-profit theatre companies do not maintain a repertory of actors. That is, they cast each play with free-lance actors.

In addition, there also exist theatre enterprises known as Equity Waivers or showcase productions. These are one-shot productions produced for a variety of reasons (to raise money, to showcase talent) for a short run and sanctioned by the unions to employ nonunion actors and technicians for little—or more often no—salary. Equity actors are also allowed to perform in these showcases, and casts almost always consist of a mix of experienced and inexperienced talent. Because these productions are generally put on to attract interest from would-be producers, they happen in New York and Los Angeles. Throughout the country, community theatres also produce theatre with nonunion actors, but this is generally considered nonprofessional theatre. Community theatre is probably the best place for virgin actors to get a taste of theatre.

It is also worth mentioning theatre activity abroad. While Actors' Equity makes it very difficult for American actors to work in Britain, some Americans are lured by the tremendous amount of theatrical activity there and do manage to secure a right-to-work card (the equivalent of our green card). The only actors allowed to work in both the United States and Britain without intense negotiating with the unions are those with international status—in other words, actors whose names are known worldwide.

Even for working actors who have already been cast in a play scheduled to move to London's West End (the equivalent of our Broadway) or one of her national theatre companies or even a fringe theatre (equivalent to our off- and off-off-Broadway), strict union rules apply. The only way such an American actor can move along with a production is if an English actor is hired for an American production, not necessarily in the same play but at the same time. The situation is worse for unemployed American actors: it is actually illegal to go to England looking for work. Still, some actors find ways around this. Some are married to English people, or have English parents, or find some way to get their right-to-work permit.

Robert Allen Ackerman, who directs both theatre and film, talks about his experience as an American director working in London:

"I love working in England because it has a real sense of a theatre community that doesn't exist in New York anymore. The theatre is very alive and active in London, so there is always a great deal of excitement around it. Actors want to work on the stage and they think of it differently than American actors. In America, the eye is always on what is coming next. So American actors often work in a play because they hope that this job will get them another job. In England, actors tend to think of getting cast in a role as the end, not as the means to the end. In England there is really a sense that theatre is a profession and that everybody is always going to work one place or another and that there are always interesting plays to do.

"English actors are always interested in playing interesting roles and they don't care where it is. Perhaps this attitude prevails for English actors because there isn't the possibility of a big movie contract at the end of a successful run. Nobody thinks that way—they just think of doing the play they are doing as well as they can. There is much more of a company feeling in England. They are a socialist country at heart regardless of what the government happens to be about at a given moment. You don't feel the separation between the people making a lot of money and the people who aren't making so much. So if you are doing a play and working with Vanessa Redgrave or any of the other great English actors, there is not a sense of status—

who has the bigger part or is making more money. Everybody is just concerned with getting the play on."

Despite the supportive atmosphere in English theatre, Ackerman says it is "not impossible but very, very difficult for young American actors to work in England." As with everything else, those who are determined find a way.

The following is a breakdown of the various theatre arenas in America, including more specific information on casting procedures.

BROADWAY

The best-known commercial theatre district in America is Broadway. Known affectionately as "the street" by theatrical professionals, Broadway consists of approximately thirty-five "legitimate" houses between Forty-first and Fifty-third streets in New York City and the plays that are presented on those stages. Broadway theatres are owned and operated by theatre organizations such as the Shubert Organization, the Jujamcyn, the Nederlander Organization, and a few independent theatre owners, dubbed "the landlords." Some well-known Broadway theatres are the Winter Garden, the Lunt-Fontanne, and the Shubert. Only union actors are allowed to perform in Broadway plays, and for the most part only actors represented by agents are ever considered for employment. The one exception to this is chorus roles. Notices of Broadway dancer/singer auditions can be found in such trade papers as Backstage.

Broadway producers rent Broadway theatres from the landlords on a per-show basis; therefore there are no on-staff casting directors or general auditions. Exceptions to this rule are the Roundabout Theatre, Circle in the Square Theatre, and Lincoln Center, not-for-profit resident theatre companies with Broadway status. In all other cases, casting is done by independent casting directors hired on a per-show basis. Some better-known casting directors who work on Broadway plays are: Billy Hopkins; Johnson Liff; Meg Simon Casting; Hughes Moss; Stuart Howard/Amy Schecter; Jay Binder Casting; Rick Shulman; and Wendy Ettinger. Addresses can be found in the Ross Reports and other trade publications.

ROAD TOURS

Just as the Shuberts and Nederlanders and independent theatre owners own and rent out theatres on Broadway, they also own and rent out commercial theatres all across the country. For the most part, these theatres house road-tour productions of successful Broadway plays. Occasionally commercial productions have a trial run before coming to Broadway, but this is not the same thing as a road tour. Preview tours were once the way all commercial theatre was produced, until it got too expensive to schlep scenery and a company around with a new production. At any rate, bus-and-truck tours are a haven for many an actor, especially if the tour is with a national company and ensures employment for months at a time.

Some commercial theatres around the country are: the Shubert (Boston and Chicago); Jones Hall in Houston; Civic Center in Syracuse; the Ordway in St. Paul; and the Ahmanson in Los Angeles. As with Broadway theatres, these commercial, legit houses do not employ an on-staff casting director. Most of the casting directors listed above as Broadway casting directors also cast road tours. Casting notices for chorus roles can be found in Backstage.

OFF BROADWAY

Off Broadway is a difficult term to define because it is a hybrid of both commercial and not-for-profit theatre. Some refer to off Broadway as a "baby Broadway" because it has become the place to take commercial productions that can't survive on Broadway, where the houses can have over a thousand seats. Commercial off-Broadway theatre is produced and cast much the same way as Broadway. Independent casting directors are retained on a per-show basis and work almost exclusively with agents, who submit clients for specific roles. Some commercial off-Broadway theatres are the Cherry Lane, the Lucille Lortel, and the Minetta Lane. Most of the casting directors previously listed under Broadway also work off Broadway.

There are a number of seasonal not-for-profit companies functioning off Broadway. Most of these began as off-off-Broadway theatre companies. When they were able to increase their funding to the point where they could pay standard minimum salaries for off Broadway, they were designated as such by the union. As a general rule, off-Broadway theatres that house a permanent company—that is, an administrative staff, production personnel, and technicians—also employ in-house casting directors. These casting directors function differently from the independent casting directors mentioned above. They hold auditions for every production their company mounts, but they also offer general auditions a few times a year to become acquainted with new talent. In addition, all theatres that produce over a season rather than per show must hold at least ten days of Equity Principal Auditions (EPAs). (Commercial producers must hold three days of EPAs for each production.) EPAs are organized through Equity and the rules concerning them change every two years. More information on EPAs and general auditions is included in chapter 5, "Trying Out." Examples of off-Broadway producing organizations are: Playwrights Horizons; The New York Shakespeare Festival; Manhattan Theatre Club; Second Stage; and Circle Repertory Company.

OFF-OFF-BROADWAY

Off-off-Broadway is a term that refers to most not-for-profit theatre activity in New York that isn't under an off-Broadway contract. Salaries are less than off Broadway, for actors as well as for everyone else, and union restrictions are less stringent. Some off-off-Broadway is produced by theatre companies, similar to off Broadway but with smaller budgets and staff, and usually without a permanent theatre. These companies were the hardest hit by the lack of government funding and several fell by the wayside during the late 1980s. Then again, new ones crop up all the time. Several—for example, Naked Angels—are considered to be on the cutting edge creatively. Naked Angels was founded by a group of young actors itching to do exciting theatre and tired of sitting around waiting to be called. Several of them, like Rob Morrow (of TV's "Northern Exposure") and Fisher Stevens, are now successful actors apart from Naked Angels. Casting opportunities are a mixed bag. In some cases casting is listed in *Backstage*; in other cases casting is by agent submissions.

REGIONAL THEATRE (RESIDENT THEATRE)

Regional theatre refers to the thriving noncommercial theatre activities outside New York City, and specifically to the resident theatre companies both inside and outside New York that are members of LORT—the League of Resident Theatres. Some of the better-known resident theatres are South Coast Repertory in Costa Mesa, California; Steppenwolf and the Goodman in Chicago; Seattle Repertory; Arena Stage in Washington, D.C.; and Actors Theatre of Louisville. Most resident theatre companies employ a casting director who holds general auditions as well as auditions for specific plays. In the second case, actors are selected from agent submissions, from "generals," and from casting directors' files. Some resident theatre company directors come to New York to cast specific roles; some cast exclusively from local talent. It should be noted that because a great number of Broadway and off-Broadway plays are first mounted in regional theatres, they get a lot of attention from New York producers. As an actor this attention means New York exposure and all that goes along with that. There are some actors who make a decent living in regional theatre and have no ambition other than to continue doing so. In any case, regional theatre is an excellent arena to work in because it allows actors to perform in both new plays and classics; to work with some fine directors; to have their work seen by professionals; and a chance to gain professional status and Equity membership. Also, as you will read below, agents and casting directors are impressed by regional theatre experience. There are several reference guides available that offer complete lists of regional theatres throughout the country. *TCG's Theatre Directory* is excellent and is published annually by Theatre Communications Group, Inc., 355 Lexington Ave., New York, NY 10017.

So many professionals in a position to employ young actors mentioned regional theatre as an alternative or adjunct to training that we are including a "Voices" section here. They all cautioned that competition is tougher than ever, but added that life away from the fast track of New York and L.A. is a better place to develop as an actor.

VOICES

Alexia Fogel, casting director: "Regional theatre is where the heart of theatre is in this country. It is where people are still doing plays too expensive to try in New York. For a young actor the best place to work after they complete their training is regional theatre. Because you have to show up eight times a week, you will really learn about the rehearsal process, you learn how to work with an audience, and you learn how to work with other people in the profession and come up with some form of diplomacy to get you through the bad days. These are important disciplines. And if you can do that, it is easier for you to step into other things. It gives you a real basis to understand how you work as an actor. You don't have that time in TV or film. Especially as a young actor, the more you work the more you get a sense of the way you work as an actor. So when you step into film and TV work, where they shoot out of sequence, or you have a different director every week, it is much easier to conjure up your talents."

Daniel Swee, casting director: "Coming to New York is not the be-all and end-all. Many theatres across the country produce high-quality theatre and provide great opportunities for actors. To become a very good actor, I advise many young actors to go to a city where it's easier to live and where there is work. The problem is that many actors now have this great impatience to make it immediately. Probably because there are so many youth-based films and television shows, there is this unrealistic need to become a star very quickly. So people get sidetracked and forget that what they wanted to do was become a good stage actor. To do that you still have to plug away for years, and while it is less apparent where the training ground is today, because everyone is doing less work, regional theatre is still the best arena."

Ed Betz, agent: "Regional theatre is a good way to get out of the city for a while. When you are just starting out, it's the experience that you are after, and you never know where these roles lead—what the director will do next, et cetera."

■

Juliet Taylor, casting director: "It is debilitating to your work to try to sell yourself before you develop as an actor. If you can't study, then find an arena to work in before the world sees you. There are actually more places to work outside of New York or Los Angeles. It is ideal to spend a period of time in regional theatre. That's what they do in England. In fact, you have to work a minimum of twenty months in English regional theatre before you can even get into British Equity."

Jim Carnahan, agent: "I love regional theatre. It is the only place you are going to play the great parts in the American theatre. It's a good idea to get those parts under your belt while you are still young. Once you come out here to L.A. it is no longer about playing the part—until you start doing leads—it's more about the money or being seen. But playing the role is what it should be about for a young actor. They hardly do the classics in New York anymore. So my advice is to try to get into drama school—Yale, Juilliard, the University of Washington—and then, unless you feel ready to go to New York, ply your trade in another big regional-theatre city like Chicago or Seattle. Of course, it's like anything else—too much of it is a bad thing. Some actors get stuck on the regional theatre treadmill and are never in town to audition for other stuff."

SUMMER STOCK

There are hundreds of summer stock theatres in operation throughout the country during the summer months. These theatres are still, as they always have been, the place from which many young actors disembark. Summer stock is where you should begin—to test your passion, to gain some street smarts, to pay your dues. In addition, summer stock offers you the chance to mingle and work with professionals, an opportunity to immerse yourself in theatre (sometimes working on as many as ten plays a summer), and it can be a bridge to cross over from nonprofessional to professional or semiprofessional work. While your first stint in summer stock may find you sweeping stages and painting sets, there is also the chance you might find yourself on stage with one or two lines to speak. Summer stock is well worth experiencing, even if your pay consists of little more than the smell of the greasepaint and the roar of the crowd.

Summer stock theatres run the gamut from the spectacular to the tacky. They fall into various categories, and these categories determine your pay and whether you need to be a member of Equity. There are Council of Stock Theatres (COST) or "star" houses; tent and musical theatres; Equity regional playhouses; and nonunion resident theatres. Applications usually require a picture and a résumé, letters of recommendation, and sometimes a vocal audition tape. Many summer stock companies throughout the country cast their plays and fill the many other technical positions through what are known as combined auditions, which are held months before the summer season, usually in February and March. In order to participate in one of these auditions (at which there will be dozens of directors and producers), you must write to the organization and request an application. Be sure to write well in advance of the audition dates. If your application goes through, you will be given an audition time. The good news is that many companies that participate will accept non-Equity performers.

The following is a list of some organizations that hold combined auditions, and addresses to which to write for an application. In addition, Theatre Directories publishes a guide, *Summer Theatre Directory*, which lists 450 summer theatres and summer training programs. It is published annually. The book is available in drama specialty bookstores or by mail: Theatre Directories, P.O. Box 519, Dorset, VT 05251, or by phone: (802) 867-2223.

BAY AREA GENERAL
AUDITIONS
Theatre Bay Area
657 Mission Street
San Francisco, CA 94105
(non-Equity)

EAST CENTRAL THEATRE
CONFERENCE
Dept. of Speech and Theatre
Montclair State College
Upper Montclair, NJ 07043

ILLINOIS THEATRE
ASSOCIATION
1225 W. Belmont
Chicago, IL 60657

INDIANA THEATRE
ASSOCIATION
Butler University Theatre
400 Sunset Avenue
Indianapolis, IN 46208
(Equity)

MICHIGAN THEATRE
ASSOCIATION
Box 762
Marshall, MI 49068
(non-Equity)

MID-AMERICAN THEATRE
CONFERENCE AUDITIONS
Dept. of Theatre and Film
University of Kansas
Lawrence, KS 60045
(non-Equity)

MIDWEST THEATRE
AUDITIONS
Webster University
470 East Lockwood
St. Louis, MO 63119

NEW ENGLAND THEATRE
CONFERENCE
50 Exchange Street
Waltham, MA 02154

NORTHWEST DRAMA
CONFERENCE
Drama Dept.
Washington State University
Pullman, WA 99164-2432
(non-Equity)

OHIO THEATRE ALLIANCE
405 N. Park Street
Columbus, OH 43215
(Equity and non-Equity)

OUTDOOR DRAMA
AUDITIONS
Institute of Outdoor Drama
CB 3240, NCNB Plaza
University of North Carolina
Chapel Hill, NC 27559
(non-Equity)

SOUTHEASTERN THEATRE
CONFERENCE
506 Striling Street
University of North Carolina
at Greensboro
Greensboro, NC 27412
(Equity and non-Equity)

SOUTHWEST THEATRE
ASSOCIATION
Route 1, Box 139
Waedler, TX 78959
(Equity and non-Equity)

STRAW HAT AUDITIONS
Box 1226
Port Chester, NY 10573
(non-Equity)

VERMONT ASSOCIATION
OF THEATRES
VATA Auditions
Box 93
Dorset, VT 05251
(non-Equity)

WISCONSIN THEATRE
AUDITIONS
Continuing Education
for the Arts
Room 726
Lowell Hall
610 Langdon Street
Madison, WI 53703
(non-Equity)

DINNER THEATRE

Dinner theatres are located all over the country, often in the suburbs or in rural communities where no other theatre exists. There are dinner-theatre chains and those that are independently owned. Dinner theatre is not the place to work if you are interested in doing new plays or classic theatre; light comedies and musicals are favorites. Most productions are "packaged in"—that is, produced else-where—and moved intact. There are non-Equity and Eq-uity dinner theatres. Auditions are posted in the trades. Most actors look at dinner theatre as a means to an end, a way to get some experience and credits to add to your résumé and to pay the rent. Non-Equity dinner theatres are always less professional than Equity dinner theatres, and you may be expected to wait on tables between shows—and, in fact, be satisfied with a salary composed of tips! Obviously, dinner theatre is hardly a place to get discovered, but it can be a start, especially if you have few credits. For more information on dinner theatre you can write to the National Dinner Theatre Association, Box 726, Marshall, MI 49068.

THEME PARKS

Theme parks such as Disney World, Disneyland, and Great Adventure are more popular than ever and offer employment opportunities for thousands of actors, singers, dancers, and musicians. Several of these enterprises put on fully staged productions and their facilities are often state of the art. On the positive side, theme parks offer decent salaries as well as benefits. The bad news is that you often have to commit yourself to a seven- or twelve-month contract. Again, this venue, like dinner theatre, should be viewed as a way to gain experience and earn income. Because of the long-term commitment, theme parks are less appealing. Auditions are listed in the trade papers and are held cross-country. Theme parks and show producers often hold joint auditions. Below is a list of producers and theme parks for you to contact with regard to audition guidelines.

Theme Parks and Show Producers:

Inquiries should be marked to the attention of the Entertainment Department.

ALLAN ALBERT
PRODUCTIONS, INC.
561 Broadway, Suite 10C
New York, NY 10021
(212) 966-8881

ATF ENTERTAINMENT,
LTD.
P.O. Box 090039
Brooklyn, NY 11209-0001
(718) 745-4794

BUSCH ENTERTAINMENT
CORP.
One Busch Gardens Blvd.
Williamsburg, VA 23187-8785
(804) 253-3300

WALT DISNEY WORLD
P.O. Box 10,000
Lake Buena Vista, FL
32830-1000
(407) 345-5755

KINGS PRODUCTIONS
1932 Highland Ave.
Cincinnati, OH 45219
(513) 241-8989

MOLONEY PRODUCTIONS
2883 Wilder Rd.
Metamora, MI 48455
(313) 667-3811

PAUL OSBORNE'S
PARK SHOWS
5118 Goodwin Ave.
Dallas, TX 75206
(214) 824-0128

SHOW BIZ
INTERNATIONAL, INC.
5142B Old Boonville
Highway
Evansville, IN 47715
(812) 473-0880

SIX FLAGS CORP. SHOW
PRODUCTIONS
1168 113th St.
Grand Prairie, TX 75050
(214) 988-8332

Parent companies for various theme parks:

ASTROWORLD
90001 Kirby Dr.
Houston, TX 77054
(713) 794-3232

BUSCH GARDENS—
THE DARK CONTINENT
P.O. Box 9158
Tampa, FL 33674-9158
(813) 985-4235

DISNEYLAND
1313 Harbor Blvd.
Anaheim, CA 92803
(714) 490-3126

WALT DISNEY WORLD/
EPCOT CENTER
P.O. Box 10,000
Lake Buena Vista, FL
32830-1000
(407) 345-5755

HERSHEYPARK
100 West Hersheypark Dr.
Hershey, PA 17033
(714) 534-3847

SEA WORLD

California:
1720 S. Shores Rd.
San Diego, CA 92109
(619) 222-6363

Florida:
7007 Sea Harbor Dr.
Orlando, FL 32821
(407) 351-3600

Texas:
10500 Sea World Dr.
San Antonio, TX 78251
(512) 523-3300

Ohio:
1100 Sea World Dr.
Aura, OH 44202
(216) 562-8101

INDUSTRIAL SHOWS
Large corporations often produce live multimedia theatre
to introduce a new product line to salespeople and clients.
The shows can last from a couple of days to a week or
several weeks if it is a touring show. Some production
companies specialize in producing industrial shows, but
generally auditions are posted in the trades. Most industrial shows are musicals. While you might feel foolish
dancing and singing your heart out to promote a new lip-
stick or a line of frozen foods, industrials generally pay
well and give you an opportunity to meet other professional actors. Sometimes stars who have become identi-
fied with the company's product through TV commercials
work in industrial shows.

CHILDREN'S AND EDUCATIONAL THEATRE
Several theatre companies in the country specialize in
producing plays that have special appeal and relevance
to the young. Some are commercial; others are funded.

Some maintain a resident company of actors; others hire on a project-to-project basis. Some are part of a larger producing organization. Again, auditions are posted in the trades or sometimes in local papers. There are also "arts-in-education" organizations that perform various services for young audiences, such as enrichment programs, teaching through the arts, or even therapy through the arts. For a list of such organizations contact the local branch of your library, or, if you are in New York, the Performing Arts Library at Lincoln Center.

COMEDY CLUBS

Over the past few years, comedy clubs have boomed. Clubs are everywhere, not just Los Angeles and New York, home of premium clubs like Catch a Rising Star and Caroline's. There are even comedy-club chains like Funny Bones, which has its headquarters in St. Louis. There has always been a crossover from stand-up comedy to film and television, but now more than ever comedians are employed as actors. Roseanne Arnold, Eddie Murphy, Jerry Seinfeld, Lily Tomlin, Richard Pryor, and Billy Crystal are examples of actors who began as stand-up comics. Because the networks are casting comedians in situation comedies, more and more talent scouts frequent these clubs, making them a viable arena for actors with comedic talent. Starting a career in comedy is not easy, and gaining attention can take years. As comic Merrie Ann Milwe says, "If you are thinking about a career in comedy, also think about working the road," which means years of hard work and grueling travel around the country.

There are two kinds of comedy clubs: showcase clubs and road clubs. Showcase clubs tend to be located where the talent scouts are, in Los Angeles and New York. Road clubs are found all over the country. Showcase clubs run the gamut from amateur status to headline status. Generally in an evening, three to six comics perform ten to forty minutes of material in succession. Some of the better clubs, once known for developing new talent, now feature only headliners and midlevel acts; some still function as a breeding ground for emerging talent, and some even hold amateur contests. The pay ranges from cab fare (for amateurs) to thousands of dollars for headline comics. The road clubs, many of which are part of national chains, tend to pay less to headliners and more to new comics with some showcase experience.

Auditions for showcase clubs almost always take place in front of an audience—generally on Sunday or Monday evenings, traditionally slow nights. New comics are required to prepare five to ten minutes of material and then sink or swim. As with casting directors, there are sympathetic and unsympathetic bookers—some will take the time to give you honest feedback, others won't. It is not unusual to be asked back to audition several times before being invited to return as a regular. To audition for road clubs that are part of a chain, it may be necessary to visit the chain's headquarters. If they like your audition, they may start you out at one of their "C" clubs; if a manager reports back favorably, you'll be booked in a better club. A helpful publication is The Comedy U.S.A. Industry Guide published by Barry Weintraub, a San Francisco comic, a "Who's Who" of clubs, performers, agents, and managers.

FILM

You are not alone if your heart's desire is to act in films. Actress Ally Sheedy explains part of the allure: " . . . it is rewarding to do film because it is so intimate. The camera is right there, and that is a very special kind of feeling."

Some of you may be so eager to take the first plane out to Hollywood that you've skipped the previous pages of this book, which concentrate on theatre. Well, turn back and read from the beginning, because with few exceptions, to have a successful, enduring film career you should have theatre experience. The reasons are several.

There is no provision in the Screen Actors Guild contract—as there is with the theatre union Equity—making it mandatory for producers to have open calls for union actors when they are casting a film. The open calls that are held are few and far between.

What does happen when a studio or production company is casting a feature film? The casting people will contact a breakdown service—describing in detail the roles that are being cast—to be sent around to agents. The agents in turn will submit their clients. It is rare that a casting director will see an unrepresented actor, one who doesn't have an agent. In Hollywood, where most films are cast, it is impossible to get an audition without an agent. As you will read in chapter 8, the way to get an agent is by working in theatre or attending one of the prestigious theatre schools that participate in the presentations.

We have already emphasized the benefits of stage training. However, many young actors want to go directly into the film industry, and although everyone we conferred with advises against it, some actors have managed to accomplish the seemingly impossible. Generally, actors who start their careers in Hollywood cut their teeth in television, doing small roles in TV movies of the week (MOWs), episodic TV, and TV commercials. A casting director for a company that casts film extras recalls pulling Bruce Willis's picture out of the active files when he was hired to star in the TV pilot for the series "Moonlighting."

Within a few months he went from extra to star—although, of course, he spent years before that paying his dues.

No discussion of the film industry can exclude the subject of Hollywood, because that is where the action is. Films are also made in New York, but only a fraction compared to Los Angeles. Few films are shot completely in New York; because of the high expense, some producers opt to film "establishing shots" in New York, which give a film a New York look, and then finish the film elsewhere, like Canada or North Carolina, where wages and living conditions are cheaper. To go to Hollywood or not is an age-old conflict with actors of varying accomplishment. Here it is best to listen to the voices of the experts, whose opinions vary and in some cases are self-contradictory . . .

Self-contradiction exists because Hollywood itself is a paradox: a place where an untrained actor with the right look can become a star overnight, and at the same time a place where no one will talk to you until you have credits, training, and an agent. Ironically, some actors move to Los Angeles only to find themselves auditioning for plays just to gain the attention of agents and casting directors who could call them in for film auditions! But beware—there is plenty of theatre activity in L.A., but it does not stir the professional community with the same interest found in New York, where casting people really do scour theatre for new talent. As with most things, in weighing a move to L.A., listen to what people in the know say, add in your own particulars (you believe you have the right look for the movies; you prefer living in California; you hate New York or some other city), and come up with the choice that is right for you.

VOICES

Robert Allan Ackerman, a director who has worked in New York and Los Angeles as well as England, Japan, France, and Israel: "As astounding as it sounds, even to me, I find myself telling young actors to go to Los Angeles because there is work there. New York can be very depressing, because there is just not enough work to go around.

"An interviewer once asked the late Joe Papp how he felt about all these playwrights, directors, and actors abandoning New York for Hollywood. He said something like 'Animal life has always gone where there is food and water,' and of course he was right. Young actors used to be able to survive in New York, get a rent-controlled apartment and earn enough money to pay for lessons. They would go to Joe Allen's restaurant and know everybody —some people were making money and some weren't, but everybody was doing something. There was a tremendous community of actors in New York when I was starting out. Now all the people I started out with live in Los Angeles.

"Ideally actors should be able to go back and forth between theatre and film, New York and L.A. They certainly do in England, but in England all actors are trained for the stage. I still believe young actors starting out should be working on the stage—although ultimately some actors who are wonderful film actors can never be great stage actors and vice versa. Young actors need to know that what happens to you in the movies is you generally are typecast. The intimacy of the camera makes personality and small behavioral things become what people like about you and expect to see from you. You don't get to stretch . . . the way you do in the theatre. The young actors I meet today spend a lot of energy on getting TV series and soap operas because they want to make a lot of money very quickly. That wasn't the case when I was starting out. We were more interested in being good—the idea of going on a series would have been like tying our hands and feet. The truth is that you can make a lot of money in L.A. An actor can get attached to the right series and make a fortune before you know it. Unfortunately, some actors lose the impulse for quality when the quick millions start pouring in."

Jim Carnahan, an L.A.-based talent agent who has worked in New York: "It is very different for actors in Los Angeles and New York. As an agent, one of the hardest things for me to get over is that in L.A. they don't always go with the best actor, but will choose the actor who is more charismatic. In New York, ninety percent of the time it is about who gives the best audition; out here it is about who gives the best audition thirty percent of the time. It is less about talent out here and more about a combination of talent, looks, timing, TV-Q [a measuring system of how well audiences know and like you]. The problem is there isn't enough work in New York anymore. All the TV and film work has come out here, so I find many actors, directors, writers have also come out here to make a living. But for young actors I still have an old-fashioned belief in New York first. There is so much to learn . . . in New York that actors don't learn in Los Angeles. Also, it is less personal out here. In New York there are maybe forty major casting directors, if even that many. Out here, there are probably two hundred and fifty casting directors, and even if they adore an actor they can only bring him in two times a year because the film people only work on two or three movies a year. In New York, good casting directors work on several plays a year, and if they like you they can generate enough activity so that you would be likely to get a job where an agent can see you. The business is so much bigger in Los Angeles, it is harder for a young actor to get a foothold. But young people continue to come out here.

"I think the whole 'Brat Pack' thing did something to young actors. They saw all these kids making a fortune doing films. In the fifties all the actors that made it big here, even James Dean, came out of the 'Studio,' and so New York was important. The last influx of stars didn't come out of New York, so New York and theatre and doing good work became less important.

"The thing young actors need to be aware of is how easy it is to step into an unreal world out here. Anything can happen. We had a client who got a starring role in a TV series on her third professional audition. But what will happen to her after the show is canceled is the question. How well will she be prepared to go on? Not as well, I can assure you, had she had tons of theatre experience behind her. When you are a young actor, it should be the time to do wonderful roles, with character arcs, because you won't have that chance again until you start playing leads."

There is more work for actors in Los Angeles, but better opportunities to build a solid foundation for a career in New York and regional theatre. Hollywood can be dangerous for young actors, because along with instant fame sometimes comes spiraling failure. Like Icarus, who flew so high that the sun melted his wings, many a young TV or film star plummeted and was left wingless after premature success. Actor James McDaniel had substantial theatre credits before he made his first trip to L.A. Like a lot of New York actors (a term that translates as "actors with stage experience"), he is grateful he spent years toiling in the theatre before going to work in Hollywood.

■

James McDaniel: "I am so happy I came straight to New York when I decided to become an actor instead of going to L.A. If I went to L.A. I wouldn't be in this business. The respect for the craft is quite different in L.A. People get into the movies because they want to be famous. They don't have a clue as to what a stage actor's process is about. When I was a regular on a TV series ["Cop Rock"] I spent a lot of time in L.A. and met a lot of actors who wanted advice. They didn't know how to break down a scene or do more than come in and say lines. I went to a restaurant with a friend of mine and the waitress said she was an actress. She was doing a workshop—they all do these workshops, not for the work but hoping to be seen by casting people. We asked her about the play, who wrote it, what it was about. Well, she says, I don't really know because I am just doing this one scene. You see, she hadn't even read the play. This is so off-base for someone who has come from a stage background. But out there it is perfectly fine. Not everyone is like that. The series I was in had a great ensemble, cast mostly from New York, and everybody meshed, we all talked the same language."

A lot of New York actors don't trust or understand Los Angeles. One actress told us she feels like some "kook" whenever she goes to L.A. because "there is no room for eccentricity there—everything is based on appearance."

Hollywood can be a confusing and frustrating town filled with traps, especially for the young and inexperienced actor. As you read earlier, B. D. Wong decided to go to Los Angeles a year after starting his career in New York because he felt it was time to make a move. By religiously reading audition notices in *Backstage*, he had managed in New York to get chorus work and his Equity card, but no speaking parts. He moved to Los Angeles. Once there, he found L.A. such a pleasant place to live that he became more interested in the beach than his ca-

reer! Deciding "good karma" was all he needed, B. D. went
through what he calls his "lazy period." Luckily, he got
over his laid-back L.A. attitude quickly, by taking classes
and finding an agent who began sending him out on auditions. The point is, with its perfect weather, fantasy-
land milieu, and something-will-happen-tomorrow am-
bience, Hollywood can turn the most ambitious actor into
a beach bum.

There are other traps in Hollywood. By now you should
realize the most important thing for young actors is to
work—in drama school, summer stock, regional theatre,
off and off-off-Broadway, films—whatever you can get.
Work begets more work. For the unknown actor, Hollywood can turn into one big waiting room where time goes
by and the jobs never appear. Even actors with credits find
it frustrating waiting for the right job to come along. Jason
Alexander returned to New York after appearing in the
film *Pretty Woman* because although he constantly heard
"We love ya" and "You're beautiful," the jobs didn't come
with enough rapidity to suit him. His bread and butter
was in New York—and even after *Pretty Woman* he came
back and continued to do commercial voice-overs and theatre. He didn't return to Los Angeles until he got a solid
job offer—as "George" on the television sitcom "Seinfeld."

Agent Ed Betz believes it is a smart move to go out to
L.A. and accumulate as much film footage as possible
"doing episodics, small roles in films, and movies of the
week" because "Los Angeles is where all the real money
is and where all the real work is."

Of all the people who spoke to us about the question
of moving to Hollywood, the most sensible advice came
from casting director Alexia Fogel. Specifically discussing
pilot season, which is late fall through April, the network
casting director said: "Actors should stay in the place they

feel comfortable. If you want to go to L.A. during pilot season because it is easier to drive to an audition than it is to be put on tape in New York, then go. If you like living in New York, surrounded by all its energy, then don't go. We have cast a lot of people off of tape. In fact, for the past few years almost half the roles of every pilot season have come out of New York. Your spirit begins to break between auditions and your acting changes when you are in a city you don't want to be in."

Ultimately, every actor who wants to work in film will have to consider a trip to Los Angeles. But early in your career, it seems you should only head west if that is where you want to live, where you feel comfortable and can be productive. Another matter for you to consider before going to L.A. is how compatible your values are with Hollywood's. As Ally Sheedy told us, "Success is measured differently in New York and Hollywood. In L.A. it is all about dollar signs." Some actors can't stand it. Others thrive on it, or at least learn to cope.

Just as there are various categories of theatre, there are categories of film.

FEATURE FILMS

A feature film is by definition any film of feature length (ninety minutes to three hours) that is made for entertainment purposes. Feature films are made for theatrical release, that is, to be shown in movie theatres, or elsewhere (television, cable, home video). Features made specifically for network television are known as MOWs (movies of the week). Big-budget theatrical movies tend to come out of Hollywood, produced by Hollywood producers and distributed by one of the major studios (Warner Bros., Paramount Communications, Universal, Columbia, Tri-Star, Disney, Twentieth Century Fox). Casting is done either by independent casting directors hired on a per-picture basis or by studio casting departments. When a studio or production company is casting a feature film, the casting directors, either independent or on staff, contact a breakdown service and describe in detail the roles that are being cast. The breakdown service sends the role descriptions to agents. The agents in turn will submit their clients. It is rare that a film-casting director will see an actor not represented by an agent, especially in Hollywood. Many of the studios maintain New York casting offices as an adjunct to their Los Angeles offices. New York film-casting directors do cover theatre to keep up on emerging talent. If they especially like an actor, they may call him in just to meet him, even if there is no project upcoming. Independent casting directors are known to move around with a picture, setting up office wherever the production is shooting, even on location. The best way to locate an independent casting director's immediate address is to visit the local SAG office, where a listing of films in production is usually posted in the members' lounge. Also, city and state film commission offices often prepare a weekly list of films shooting in town. These lists usually include the addresses of the production offices. As far as studio casting departments, all you need is the studio address and the words "feature-casting department" to forward your picture and résumé. Most Hollywood films come packaged with stars in place before a casting director starts to work. But when a newcomer is needed, the casting people get busy searching— again, mostly through agents, but on rare occasions self-submissions catch a casting director's fancy. It is always a good idea to send your picture and résumé to film-casting directors every six months or so, because generally they work on a few films a year.

One feature film opportunity sometimes open to non-union actors is work as an extra. Some casting directors

specialize in this area of casting. In New York, Sylvia Fay
and Joy Todd are two such casting directors. For up-to-
date listings throughout the country, see the *Ross Reports
U.S.A.* and *Ross Reports Television*; also, contact your
local SAG office. From time to time extra-casting directors
hold open auditions—they do this mostly because SAG
requires them to (SAG doesn't have the same requirement
for principal casting directors)—but sometimes they need
a large number of actors for a crowd scene. The open calls
are always advertised in the trade papers. Bring your picture and résumé or you will be wasting your time, and be
prepared for a long day.

TV SERIES

While MOWs are cast the same way feature films are, by
independent casting directors or by the studio casting department, television series are usually cast by the network
(ABC, NBC, CBS, Fox) that is producing the series, sometimes in conjunction with the production company. (Some
TV shows and MOWs are produced solely by the networks;
most are coproduced with a production company, such as
Warner Bros. Television.) The majority of TV shows are
produced in Los Angeles, but most of the networks maintain a New York casting office. Because there is still cachet
in being a New York actor, most L.A. TV producers insist
on seeing New York actors when auditioning for a prime-
time series pilot. A pilot is the first episode of a TV series
and traditionally is very carefully produced because it is
used to sell the show to potential advertisers. (Recently
the networks have been looking for other, less expensive
methods of developing new shows. One method is to create theatre workshops out of potential series ideas; NBC
started a workshop in a New York theatre and hired actors
to experiment with scenes for a possible series.) Traditionally, actors have flocked to Los Angeles for the pilot

season. Auditions are also conducted in New York, put on tape, and sent to the producers in L.A. (The TV producer, as opposed to a film or theatre producer, is very much involved with casting, functioning more like the director does in the other media.) Unfortunately, as with features, almost all series work is handled through agents. Because agents earn a great deal of money when one of their clients is hired for a TV series, they are even more zealous about getting their clients jobs. Still, New York network casting people can be spotted all over town in theatres, keeping track of developing actors' work. Also, they do have general interviews with actors just to meet them, rather than audition them for a specific role. The *Ross Reports*, which are published monthly, list network casting contacts. (They are published by Television Index, Inc., 49–29 27th Street, Long Island City, New York 11101, and are also available at the AFTRA office and drama specialty bookstores.)

SOAP OPERAS

Most soaps currently running on television are still produced in New York, although some are produced in Los Angeles. Casting is done through the networks, but not by the prime-time casting directors—each soap has its own casting directors—or by the advertising agency that sponsors the show. The *Ross Reports* list the names and addresses of soap opera–casting personnel. Most of them have a "don't come or phone" policy for obvious reasons, and the amount of casting they are doing at any time depends on: the story line; their need for new actors to play new parts, or to replace actors that are leaving the show; and the number of extras they require. Although it helps to have an agent submit you, it is not as essential as it is for feature or prime-time auditions. The straightforward approach can work—a letter submitted with your picture and résumé, asking for an interview at the casting director's convenience. It is a good idea to watch the soaps, to see what the story line is and what types of actors are being used, in order to gauge your own possibilities of being cast. Although soaps still tend to cast actors with traditional good looks, there is more room for ethnic actors, and sometimes even a quirky, off-beat character is written into a script.

A note of caution: Soap opera—casting directors often ask you to "cold read" a script without allowing for preparation. This is rarely done in other types of auditions, except for commercials. There was a time that serious actors wouldn't be caught dead in a soap opera. Today that is no longer true. Why, even the late Dame Judith Anderson, considered by some to be one of our greatest actresses, appeared in the soap "Santa Barbara" for several seasons. Other known stars have also made guest appearances, and more than a few actors crossed over from soaps into prime-time television and films. With the lack of training grounds for young actors today, soap operas are considered a perfectly legitimate arena in which to start a career. With that in mind, you don't have to look at soap opera work as the end of the line, especially if you continue to take classes to keep your skills well honed. Also on the positive side is that soaps pay a solid and steady salary. But don't think the work is easy—it isn't.

COMMERCIALS

On-camera TV commercial work and off-camera voice-overs are two ways an actor can make the system support him. Many young actors go through a period when they think that doing commercials is selling out, prostituting their artist's soul. But they usually find themselves broke and have to add some realism to their idealism. Working in commercials, especially for those with serious drama school training, is a difficult transition to make—but transitions are what actors are paid to do, in one form or another. There was a time when known actors wouldn't appear in commercials. Twenty years ago, as a commercial casting director trainee, one of us recalls being asked to prepare a list of "stars" willing to endorse products. The list had five names on it. That same year, however, unknowns like Lily Tomlin, Kenny Rogers, and little Brooke Shields happily auditioned for us. Today there is little prejudice against commercial work among celebrities unless they find the product or the advertising disreputable.

The money, especially for a national spot, can keep an actor solvent for months or even years. Ally Sheedy, Jason Alexander, and James McDaniel all began their careers doing commercials and used the money they earned to further their careers by taking classes and appearing in theatre workshops. The exposure of a well-produced commercial has gained more than one actor his agent. And the experience of being on a set and working with the camera is clearly beneficial.

TV commercials are produced by commercial production companies for advertising agencies that act on behalf of their business clients. Most spots are written by an ad agency copywriter and are bid out to a number of production companies that specialize in producing commercials. Once a production company has been chosen, the spot is handed over to its producer and director. Until recently, casting was handled by the advertising agency. Now, all but a few have closed their casting departments, and casting is handled by independents. The large advertising agencies that maintain casting departments have several people to handle general casting, celebrity casting, children, models, hand and feet models, and voice-overs. Names and addresses can be found in the Ross Reports. Most commercial casting directors work exclusively with agents, but commercial agents are generally more approachable than talent agents. A listing of commercial talent agents can also be found in the *Ross Reports*.

Because commercial work generates so much money, it also generates shady practices on every level. The trades are filled with ads calling for "New Faces," or "Success in TV Commercials Now!" Trips to such offices are as productive as answering those "instant winner" letters you receive in the mail, and more expensive even than calling the 900 number required to receive the winnings. If someone claiming to be an agent or manager offers to represent you, *there is no reason for you to pay them a dime up front.* Their income should come from commissions earned on work you obtained through them.

Another scam recently discovered in the lucrative world of TV commercials is that some talent agents in New York have been charging nonunion actors higher commissions than state law allows. Actors represented by SAG, AFTRA, or Equity may not be charged more than 10 percent by an agent. But many agents take 15 to 25 percent off the top of nonunion actors' paychecks. Since most nonunion work is primarily in TV commercials, agents in this area need to be scrutinized even more than others. All talent agencies must be franchised by the three actors' unions and must follow strict rules; in New York, agencies are also required to be licensed by the city. Beware of any that are not. As you will see later, personal managers aren't monitored at all, and unscrupulous managers find ways to cheat, like asking for a fee to arrange for photographs or for keeping you in their files. This is absolutely improper. A legitimate manager may send you to a commercial agent who in turn gets you a job—in that case the manager is entitled to a fee, but certainly no more than 20 percent of your earnings for that particular job. Commercial work for actors is available in New York, Los Angeles, and Florida, although most national commercials are cast in New York and L.A.

INDUSTRIAL FILMS

For the same reasons they produce industrial shows, the business community produces industrial films: to generate business; as a public service; and for training purposes. Industrials are worthwhile to pursue because they often feature nonunion actors and the pay can be decent. You're not going to be discovered by an agent or casting director from your work—industrials are shown to non-theatrical audiences of businesspeople—but you'll have an opportunity to be around the set and become comfortable with the camera and lights. Learning set etiquette and how to be unruffled in front of the camera is worth the trouble of playing the role of an earnest car salesman or the like.

STUDENT FILMS

Here again, it is best to look at work on a student film as preparation for better things. There is usually no pay and your director will be a film student. But you'll learn how you appear on film, how to apply your skills, and how to relate to the camera. Most student film projects are limited to a month of shooting, so you won't have to commit yourself for more time than that. (If you are asked to, say no.) Roles are posted in the trades and on university bulletin boards. It is a good idea to narrow your search to the better film programs—like NYU Film School in New York and USC in California—where the students are serious and may even have a future in the business.

4
Trying Out

Being an actor and being able to handle the business part of being an actor are two very different things. You fall in love with acting, then suddenly you have to go out and attack a sometimes ruthless business that has nothing to do with what you love to do. All this presenting of yourself is a whole different ballgame than acting. —Juliet Taylor, casting director

Learning that everyone hates looking for a job should at least make you feel better. To further ease your pain, we should add that casting directors and directors don't love the audition process any more than actors. Trying to convey all that you are in a five-minute interview or audition is tough on everyone. We polled a lot of people on this issue, and on one thing they all agree: The more you audition, the better you'll audition.

Meanwhile, there are ways to prepare yourself. The most important is to understand the casting procedure. There are different kinds of auditions and interviews, and it is helpful to understand that in many cases, you will simply be meeting a casting director rather than auditioning for a specific role. Don't let the word "simply" mislead you however, because an interview can be as important to your career as an audition. The more interviews you have, the more auditions you are likely to have. The more auditions you have, the more jobs you'll get.

The casting community is a small one and is based on a mutual objective between actor and casting director: it is your job to meet them; it is their job to become familiar with your work. Knowing your work, they can present you to the director, who always has the final say with regard to casting. Casting directors want you to be good because it makes them look good.

Once you recognize the casting director/actor relationship as a professional, sympathetic one instead of an antagonistic one, your auditioning technique will improve. This is not an easy concept to learn—being judged can make most of us defensive—but it is crucial to your future as an actor. Perhaps hearing what casting directors have to say on the subject will shed some warming light. Admittedly, not all casting directors are as sensitive as the ones presented here—you are more likely to meet discourteous or harried casting directors than otherwise—but it should help to know that the really good ones are on your side. As casting director Juliet Taylor told us: "Most good casting directors are good not merely because they are able to sense what an actor's impact is going to be on an audience, but because they enjoy people and are interested in people and are able to put their own egos aside and be receptive."

VOICES

Marion Dougherty

*Marion Dougherty is the vice president of talent at Warner
Bros. casting and is credited not only for discovering such
actors as Robert DeNiro, Dustin Hoffman, Al Pacino, Robert Redford, and Jon Voight (among others), but also for
changing the role of the film-casting director. Before Marion Dougherty, casting directors were glorified secretaries
with little impact. Since Marion Dougherty, good casting
directors are recognized for their contribution. Juliet Taylor, a former assistant of Marion Dougherty's and now a
prominent casting director, told us: "Marion made the
casting director someone directors could lean on for advice . . . we all owe her a great deal of gratitude, actors
as well." Never one to hold back her opinion, Marion
introduced the concept of "arguing" over casting choices
with directors. Her ripostes in defense of actors are leg-
endary in Hollywood.*

"When I meet an actor for the first time I allow fifteen
minutes for the interview, because it usually takes five
minutes for the actor to get over the fright at seeing this
ogre. So I try to chitchat and try to make them feel at home.
That is why I have this messy office; I want it to be homey
rather than scary. I try to put them at ease because if they
are not comfortable they are not going to give their best
reading. If I give them a scene to read, I make sure to make
eye contact with them and give them something to play
off of. The trick is to give them support and try to get them
to focus, but not to give too much so that you take the
glory away from them when reading for a director.

"With unknown people I will read with them myself before calling them back to read for the director. When the role is a lead and the actor is unknown I might call them back two or three times before introducing them to the director. In the end you have to go with the director's vision because that is what needs to be on the screen. I could give a director a wonderful actor, but if he or she doesn't see it, it ain't gonna work. You can argue with a director and sometimes they come around, but sometimes they don't.

"I want actors to understand that each time I call them in, I learn something about them I could use in the future. I've called very good actors in for three or four different films and they're just not totally right, but I like them as actors and want to use them. Actors are very sensitive and they feel rejection easily. But if an actor is called back several times or for several different pictures, they should be flattered, because that casting person wouldn't call them back if they didn't believe something was there. I brought Pacino in several times before I found the right niche for him; I cast him in his first movie.

Casting directors must have a broad knowledge of a whole lot of different actors—it is our responsibility to know them and to know what they can do. Another reason we read people again and again is to give them a whack at something new—sometimes it works and sometimes it doesn't. Good casting directors try different things; if we didn't you'd get the old studio way of casting: one from column A and one from column B. I try to keep up with it all—theatre, film, and even television, which I am not terribly fond of—just so I can haul these kids in and meet them."

Alexia Fogel

*Alexia Fogel is director of casting for ABC in New York,
and she oversees all prime-time casting for pilots and
movies of the week; most times she is working on several
projects at once. She works in conjunction with ABC's
L.A. casting department and if an independent producer
is involved with a project, that company's casting director
also. Alexia Fogel came to ABC after working as a casting
director for several regional theatres, which is what prepared her for the enormous volume of work involved in
prime-time casting.*

"The hardest thing an actor has to do is walk through that
door for an interview or an audition. When a casting director forgets that, it is time for them to stop being a casting
director. It is my job to remember how difficult that is for
an actor and try to make them as relaxed as possible under
the circumstance.

"I think if actors understood the hierarchy of the people
involved in the casting process they would be less intim-
idated by casting directors. As a casting director I am a
middleman between the acting community and the
director—and in television, the writer/producer, because
the producer often is the writer of the show and also functions the way a director does in film or theatre in that he
or she is very involved with casting. Casting directors actually have far less power than actors believe. Yes, I can
help an actor get an audition and I have opinions and
freely give them, but I do not make decisions by myself.
My job in this process is to know an actor's work. I want
them to succeed and I'm certainly not challenging them
when they come in.

"It is not good enough for me to know an actor's work
only from what I've seen in my office. I have to know an

actor's body of work and see it as it changes. Which is why I go to the theatre all the time and will see an actor in four, five, six different plays. I note how he or she changes and grows. Most conscientious casting directors do that because actors' talents constantly change and grow based on their life experience, work, and age, and you have to keep up with them."

Daniel Swee and Janet Foster

Daniel Swee was casting director for the influential New York producing company Playwrights Horizons and Janet Foster was his assistant. They have given hundreds of actors their first visible exposure. Once or twice a year they conduct general auditions to which they invite actors who interest them—either from a picture and résumé, a recommendation, a school presentation, or a performance. Sometimes the waiting list for these "generals" is as long as two years, but with Daniel's sphere of influence and astute casting abilities, the wait is worth it. Daniel Swee moved on to be the casting director at Lincoln Center Theatre. Janet Foster is still at Playwrights. Both have extensive theatre backgrounds. Since they often finished each other's sentences, we are presenting their voices as one.

"It is always surprising to us that actors don't understand that casting is a subjective process, that we base our choices of who is right for a project on talks with the playwright, the director, the artistic director. Actors read this brief little breakdown and say, 'I'm bold but vulnerable—why didn't they call me in for this?' The casting director doesn't have the final say as to who gets the job. It's a filtering system—we suggest and advise and lobby and push and have a point of view, but ultimately there are many variables that go into the final choice, variables that they don't know about and have no control over. Actors need to know this so that the process becomes more human to them.

"Also, some actors don't audition well, but after some time working with the director their work will be fine. I want to know that so I can go to bat for them when necessary; that's why it is not enough just to see someone in my office. On the other hand, some actors do a bang-up audition and then can't sustain a performance, they can't go further. I need to know that too. One of the reasons the audition process is so long is that most directors don't want to wind up in that sort of situation.

"Auditioning is a different skill than acting. You are taking something out of context and having to make it real and appropriate in a very short time period. There is no rehearsal process, no director. It takes time to learn how to do it. The best way to learn is to do it often and try to figure out what you don't do well and work on that. Actors get better and better at it in the first two years after they get out of school. It is completely unreal and you have to suspend your disbelief. And of course it is nerve-racking and embarrassing to walk into a tiny room with four or five people staring at you, because the whole idea of being there is to get a job. It takes time for an actor to get over the sense that he or she is not in a combative position with the people on the other side of the table. Walking in is terrible. I know that and consider it my responsibility to make others comfortable.

"Actors psych themselves out so they can't do what they need to do, which is to walk in a room and be present and do their best possible work. We understand this isn't easy, but it would be easier if they understood that all the people in the room are not against them. When we bring you into a room to audition we want you to do well. We want you to get the job. If you are good, the director, playwright, artistic director is going to turn to us and say, 'Wow, who is that person? How did you know he or she was so good?' The casting director then becomes the golden child.

"We have seen so many auditions that we can tell who has done their preparation and who hasn't. Sometimes an actor has made strong choices, but it just doesn't happen, we see that they are having a bad day—like acting underwater—and we give them another chance if we think they can do better. Actors should understand it is our job to know as many actors as possible and to know their work as extensively as possible. Actors are always surprised when we bring them in to audition because of something they did three years ago. But it is our job to remember them.

"Sometimes we are desperate to be the first ones to give an actor their first job because we know how good they are, but they just aren't right for a part in the plays we are casting. One of the reasons we are casting directors is because we like actors and enjoy finding the right project for actors whose work we like. But it can take years to do that; actors should understand it is hard for us, too."

Casting directors are your link to directors. Directors ultimately decide who gets the job. Directors come into the casting procedure once the groundwork is done and the project is ready to be cast. The crucial thing to keep in mind when auditioning for a director is that he or she is looking at the total picture. You are only part of what ultimately is the director's vision of the play or film. Many pieces of the intricate puzzle have to fit—most importantly, the other actors already cast. The operative words here are not good and bad, but right and wrong—for the part and for the project. The final voice is that of a director.

Robert Allan Ackerman

Robert Allan Ackerman is primarily a theatre director, but he has directed films and continues to work in both fields. He has directed more stars than any other contemporary director, including Richard Gere, Susan Sarandon, Vanessa Redgrave, Al Pacino, Anne Bancroft, and many others. One reason actors are so eager to work with Bob is because they trust he will guide them and help them move forward, yet not interfere with the way they work. He has strong feelings about the audition process.

"I wish there was a way to convince actors not to take it personally when they don't get a job. I've turned down people who I thought were wonderful, actors I'd love to work with, who in fact went on to become very famous, and I knew they would and I regretted at the time not being able to use them. Tom Cruise auditioned for me twice for two different plays and I knew that he was a specially gifted, interesting young actor, but unfortunately wrong for the part I was casting.

"There are so many factors that go into casting a play, so many things have to be taken into account. The balance of a cast has to be exactly right and you may be too much like somebody else who happens to already be in the director's mind to play another role. You may be too tall or too short to play opposite another actor or too young, or you may come across as too intelligent or not intelligent enough. It often has nothing to do with how talented you may or may not be.

"Of course, some actors do get rejected because they are not very good, and that, too, has to be examined. I started out wanting to be an actor, but I realized I wasn't good and went on to do what I was good at.

"The most disturbing thing to a director auditioning

actors is when an actor isn't prepared, they haven't read the script and have no idea about the character. My feeling is that the more prepared an actor is when he comes in, the better. And that means prepared to do the part as they think it should be done. I don't like it when actors ask me what I want them to do. The less said, the better. If a director wants to talk to you or give you a suggestion, fine, but otherwise do it as you see fit.

"I don't really expect to see a performance when I'm auditioning actors. I'm looking much more for an honesty, a quality. Whether or not an actor has what I think is the right take on a scene doesn't influence me. I go to an audition usually as excited as the actor, because it is the first time I hear the play out loud. I learn a lot about the play from auditions. I've heard actors read scenes in a certain way that have really made me sit up and say, 'Oh, I have never thought of doing that scene that way, that is terrific.' I may not hire the actor for that part, but I'll certainly remember him and use what he taught me.

"Every director is different, of course, and that is another reality actors have to deal with. For instance, I find it off-putting when an actor comes to an audition wearing something that resembles a costume. But on the other hand, it is important not to come in looking completely opposite of the character. If you are auditioning for Emily in Our Town, don't come in dressed in punk clothing. But don't come in in a white dress with ribbons in your hair, either. I directed The Vortex, and I can't say how many people came in dressed like flappers; I just couldn't take them seriously. But there is a way of being really clever and in a way assuming the character without going to the obvious extreme. There are ways of fooling the director.

"There is a very mannish female character in The Vortex. The actress who wound up with the part [Molly Hagen] came in dressed very severely, but in a contemporary suit, with her hair pulled back. She was wearing clothes that she could have worn on the street and looked perfectly terrific in. She was very straightforward and projected incredible intelligence. She looked like the character, but it was done very subtly and cleverly rather than coming in a costume. It was such a good choice. I knew I was being manipulated, but I didn't mind because it was done with such wit and real understanding of who the character is.

"I have tremendous compassion for actors because they never know what a director wants to see. It is a matter of taste—like finding a lover—one person finds you adorable and charming and wonderful and another one doesn't. That is just part of the reality of the profession you've chosen."

KINDS OF AUDITIONS

THEATRE

Presentations: See "Training," Chapter 2.

EPAs and EPIs (Eligible Performer Auditions and Interviews)

Actors Equity requires producers to have a certain number of days set aside to interview and/or audition Equity members, and if time permits, a certain number of non-Equity actors. EPAs are really open calls, meaning anyone who arrives early enough to sign up will be seen. Commercial producers must have three days of EPAs; not-for-profit theatres that produce over a season rather than per show must have ten days of EPAs per year. Equity changes the rules for EPAs every two years, so it is best to check with them to keep current. Equity also does all the scheduling for these auditions and posts the notice announcing when they will be held. The theatre's casting director or some representative of the producer is always present. In order to participate, actors have been known to arrive at Equity at 2:00 or 3:00 A.M. to sign up. Unfortunately, there is no transfer of names, so if you don't make the list the first day you must sign up again the next. At present, the rule is that every actor gets five minutes, which means approximately eighty-four actors are guaranteed to be seen in a day. For the EPAs, actors are expected to come prepared with a monologue and a picture and résumé. As impossible as it seems, actors actually have been asked to audition for a play because of an EPA audition and occasionally have been cast. Others have at least had their pictures and résumés put in casting directors' files for future reference.

General Auditions

"Generals" differ from EPA open calls in several ways. First, casting directors decide to do them on their own initiative, and only actors who have been invited may attend generals. Also, fewer actors audition, usually around twenty a day as opposed to eighty-four at EPAs. Generals are held by not-for-profit producing organizations, like the New York Shakespeare Festival, and regional theatres throughout the country. Because these organizations produce several plays a season, casting directors need to keep current with regard to available talent. Being invited to a general audition is a real opportunity. While it will not result in an on-the-spot job offer, you are becoming part of the pool of actors whose work is recognized by casting directors. Actors get invited to generals based on varied criteria: picture and résumé; training; recommendations from agents, managers, friends, and associates; or an impressive EPA or presentation audition. By all means, send your picture and résumé to all producing organizations that hold generals, but be aware that most of them have a long waiting list and you may not get called for up to two years. In a general, actors are asked to perform one or two monologues, at least one of which is contemporary. If you are invited to a general be sure to ask what kind of monologue they want you to perform and if there are any monologues they are sick and tired of hearing. Casting directors become monologue specialists after a while, and some overused pieces of material drive them crazy.

Interviews

Interviews are the equivalent of a professional handshake in theatre casting, in that a casting director may just want to meet and talk to you about your work, training, and availability and get a sense of who you are. You probably will not be asked to read or perform a monologue at an interview, but rather just to converse. There are always exceptions to this rule, so it is best to always be prepared with a monologue. Actors are invited in for an interview for a variety of reasons: time didn't permit a general audition; the actor created a favorable enough impression at a general to warrant a longer, one-on-one visit; an L.A.- or other city-based actor is only in town for a short time; as a favor to an agent or manager; or, in the best scenario, as a prelude to an audition.

Auditions

Casting directors begin the casting process by reading the play and coming up with ideas for actors to play the roles. Then, after talking to the director and playwright, they get a clearer idea of what they are looking for and they prepare more lists of actors' names. They may go through lists they have made for other plays with similar roles; they look through *Theatre World*; they scour their own files for actors whose work they know through generals, interviews, or other plays. During this process they also send out breakdowns to agents, who then submit clients they believe are right for the part. Finally auditions are held—if not at the exact stage where the play is being produced, then at some facsimile. Most casting directors try to do as much prescreening as possible before calling an actor back to meet a director and/or playwright. Usually an actor is given the play to read and is expected to read it in its entirety, not merely his or her part. Rarely will an actor be asked to cold read pages he or she hasn't been asked to prepare, but there are exceptions—such as when a director might see you in a role other than the one for which you were called in to read. From this point on in the audition process, it is a matter of callbacks—in the beginning, to reevaluate an actor's work, to see how well an actor takes an adjustment from a director, but mostly to allow the director to assemble a cast that is balanced and complementary. Equity does set a limit on the number of times an actor can be called back before he or she must be paid.

FILM

Open Calls
While there is no EPA equivalent for film auditions, from time to time movie casting directors will hold an open call, usually to search for a specialized role, such as a young actor. Open calls are held only after every other avenue of finding an actor is exhausted. Anybody can show up at an open call, and often everybody does—hence the term "cattle call." Open calls are advertised in trade papers, newspapers, and on TV and radio. Sometimes cast-

ing directors will set up an open call at schools; according to legend Matt Dillon was found at such an event at Mamaroneck High School. Because so many nonprofessionals surface at open calls, pictures and résumés are not required. Casting directors who specialize in extra-casting also hold open calls for both union and nonunion members. Basically they are looking for specific types to keep in their files. (Principal casting directors, especially good ones, rarely "typecast," but in the world of extras, where sometimes hundreds of actors are needed for a film, it is your "type"—upscale yuppie, punk, businessperson, mafioso, etc.—that will get you the job.) Actors are required to bring a picture and résumé. Don't expect more than a "thank you" at these open calls; the casting directors see hundreds of actors a day and probably will be filing your picture instantaneously. Since extras are often required to supply their own wardrobe, it is a good idea to mention the extent of your wardrobe on your résumé (e.g., own ballgown, tuxedo, Hasidic outfit, tennis racket, etc.).

Interviews

From time to time, movie casting directors will call an actor in just to meet him, although this happens more often in New York than L.A. Most times, however, movie casting directors only interview when they are looking to fill a specific part. The interview is the first step toward landing a movie role and is much more decisive than an interview with a theatre casting director. It goes like this: A casting director will call you to his or her office to chat for the purpose of getting a take on the quality you put across. It is this "quality" that is uniquely yours that will interest the casting director—because that is the quality you will probably project on-screen. For this reason, the most oft-given piece of advice is to be yourself. Sometimes a movie casting director may give you "pages" from the script to read right then and there. Other times he or she will have you come back to read. Most times you won't be able to take the entire screenplay home to read because movie companies don't want their projects in circulation before the film is made. You will almost never be asked to perform a monologue for a film casting director. Eventually the casting director calls those actors back that he or she wants the director to meet. Some directors are very involved with the casting process; others don't show up until the finalist-selection process is down to the wire. Often you will be called back to read with an actor who is already cast in the film. Sometimes, when a director is in another town, the casting director might record your reading on video and send it off. Other occasions for a video "test" are: to see how you come off on camera if you have no screen credits (something happens when an actor's appearance is filtered through the camera; it has been called mysterious, magical, indescribable, but whatever it is, something happens), or to see the chemistry between you and another actor. Screen tests, with cameras, lights, wardrobe, and makeup, are rare and are given only when an actor (usually a woman) is up for a lead role in a big-budget film and has no screen credits or the role is a real departure from other roles—or perhaps there is a question of "how old" an actor translates on film. Julia Roberts, for example, did a screen test for *Pretty Woman* to see how she looked as a glamorous character. Movie casting directors call actors in for interviews (which may or may not turn into an audition) from four different sources: unsolicited pictures, résumés, and, in L.A., tapes; actors they have seen in plays, films, or on TV; actors recommended to them by associates, friends, and even other actors (Sandra Bernhard got her break in *King of Comedy* when another actress being interviewed for the job suggested to Cis Corman, the casting director, that she be called); and actors submitted by agents. In Los Angeles particularly, 99 percent of actors interviewed for film jobs come from the last source—agents.

TELEVISION

Commercial Auditions

In Los Angeles, all commercial auditions are handled by agent submissions. Casting directors will call agents, tell them what they are looking for, and call in those actors they are interested in. In New York, most casting directors also work through commercial agents, although some refer to *Theatre World* and keep files of actors whose faces interest them. Actors are usually given ten minutes per audition, at which time they are asked to read the commercial—sometimes cold, sometimes after having looked over the script in the waiting room. Finalists are called back to read for the agency producer, and oftentimes for the client on whose behalf the agency is making the commercial. Again, you may be put on video for convenience' sake.

Episodic, MOW, and Pilot Interviews

These interviews are handled much the same way as film interviews—in the casting director's office, beginning with a conversation, moving along to reading pages from the script, and ending with a video test and several callbacks. Casting is generally handled by several casting directors, with the head of casting responsible for movies of the week, pilots, and original casting for new characters on episodics (week to week). The staff casting director is responsible for guest characters, who appear only once on a show. Since most networks maintain casting departments on both coasts, it really isn't necessary any longer to travel to Los Angeles for pilot season (late fall through April).

Soap Operas

Every soap opera has its own casting department. Most soap opera casting is done through agent submissions, but because an actor's looks are so important in soaps, a beautiful or handsome face can get some attention. Soap opera-casting directors will ask you to read "pages" and expect you to know something about the soap and its characters.

———

AUDITIONING
SECRETS

Walk into an Interview with Purpose: Who would have thought the simple act of walking through a door into a room could be so critical? But it is, especially in L.A., where agent Jim Carnahan says: "How someone walks into the room can actually become the reason they get the job. Confidence is what makes the difference." Actors, casting directors, directors, and agents all mentioned "walking in" as a major factor, while at the same time stating all that is necessary is to be yourself—not hostile, overly friendly, outrageous, timid—just yourself. Granted, this is not easy. The best advice on how to walk into an interview came from two casting directors, Alexia Fogel and Daniel Swee, who together teach workshops for student actors. They call it the "cocktail party" technique:

"Assuming you are relatively well brought up, your parents conceivably taught you how to behave when you meet people you have never met before who you are only going to be with for three minutes or so. Well, you do the

same thing you would under those circumstances. Be po-
lite, say hello, do your thing, be pleasant, and move on.
Yes, it is unnatural, but so is a cocktail party—you just
make the best of it. You wouldn't walk into a cocktail
party with a need to show everybody you meet how wonderful you are in two minutes or less. Well, it is just as
unsettling when you walk into an interview with that
attitude."

From an actor's point of view, Jason Alexander explains
what you need to do to make walking in less intimidating:
"What you have to have inside out and backwards when
you walk through that door is a sense of self. Yes, you
have a job to do, but your first job is to connect with
another human being who happens to be a casting director.
You can't be just an actor showing up for an audition. First
you have to be a whole person being introduced to another
whole person. If five minutes after your audition you
should bump into one of the people who auditioned you
in a hallway and you don't recognize them, you know you
screwed up."

Make Strong Choices: This is another unanimous recommendation. When preparing for an audition it is best
to present your interpretation of the role rather than try
to second-guess what the director or casting director is
looking for. The truth is, they often don't know what they
are looking for until they see it. All the directors and casting directors we questioned admitted that they are en-
riched by the audition process, often because they learn
from actors' emotional character choices, including actors
who don't ultimately get the part.

Agent Ed Betz suggests this: "Figure out an angle on
your audition, a way to own the role, and make it uniquely
yours. There are going to be a hundred people auditioning,

so figure out something to make it special, that they won't forget. Be smart about your choices, but don't be wrong—you need to be intelligent about making your mark. You may want to underplay rather than overplay, because auditioning is about a suggestion of a character, not a full-blown performance. But make your intention known."

Daniel Swee also urges actors to make strong acting choices when auditioning, but cautions you to keep the choices sensible: "For the most part, when you see a good audition, it is because someone made a really strong choice, a choice based on the text, not a lunatic choice—like throwing chairs and yelling a lot—which is often made just for effect, where no one knows what you are getting at."

Jason Alexander offers some concrete pointers: "Figure out four or five things and commit to them. For instance, ask yourself what your character wants, and be specific—I want the other character to blink three times and kiss me behind my ear. Then ask yourself what is preventing that from happening—the character is too far away, or the character doesn't like me. Lastly, figure out the action verbs that will further your intent—to seduce, charm, cajole, tease, intimidate. Once you find your conflict and actions, just play those and don't worry how it is coming out, because you'll do an amazing reading."

Ally Sheedy has a healthy attitude toward making a character she is auditioning for individually her own: "When you audition you actually get to play that part for a little bit, to feel this character is mine and I am going to work on it and go in this direction. It may not be the way they want it, but it is a choice." Ally added this comment, which leads into the next recommendation: "I love it when the director actually works with you at an audition and says 'Try this or that' because then you can make adjustments."

Listen and React to Direction: It is important to begin
your audition with a strong intention, but it is equally
important to be flexible enough to make adjustments when
a casting director or director gives them. For one thing,
you show that you can take direction; for another, you
assure the director that you speak his or her language and
respect his or her conception of the character; and, lastly,
you indicate you are a skilled actor.

For Marion Dougherty, an actor's ability to adjust an
audition pattern can make the difference between getting
the job or not. "It is interesting in reading people how you
can tell if they are good or not by how well they make an
adjustment. I've cast people who have read a hundred and
eighty degrees wrong, but when I say, 'No, wait a minute,
try it again and try it this way,' they can do what you ask.
Some actors can; some will give you verbatim what you
heard before."

Director Bob Moss sympathizes with actors because, he
notes, not all directors take the time at auditions to give
suggestions. "A lot of directors will not ask an actor to do
it again. The actor comes in and reads, having made a
choice, and the director will just say no. Some directors
will only work with an actor in callbacks. An actor has to
be prepared for the fact that a lot of directors don't know
how to run an audition. Does this mean an actor shouldn't
make choices? No, you have to make choices—but you
are in a difficult situation."

B. D. Wong adds that you shouldn't put up with anything you feel is degrading. "There is nothing wrong with
saying during an audition that something doesn't feel
right. You have to find a way of saying this without coming
across a prima donna, but you can't allow yourself to be
walked all over, either. It requires a delicate balance, but
being an actor has a lot to do with balance. Obviously a
person has to be strong to be an actor, but if you are too

strong, then you aren't vulnerable enough. So you learn to use all the vulnerable things about you in the acting itself and the strength in the professional situations. You shouldn't be meek at an audition, but you shouldn't be an asshole, either."

Dress Appropriately: Most casting directors agree that costumes are out—if you are being stared at on the street, on the way to the audition, chances are you have dressed inappropriately. Still, we heard stories of actors so determined to persuade a director that they were the character that they dressed to the nines—and got the part. One actress, convinced the casting director couldn't see farther than her nose, bought herself a black wig and dressed for the part and was cast as an Italian widow in a play—sometimes it works. But in general, and especially for film interviews, dress as you normally do, but select something from your closet that is both comfortable and indicative of the character.

As Marion Dougherty says: "I don't like costumes, but if the part calls for a sexy girl, it is sort of stupid to come in wearing a muumuu; and if you are coming in to play a high-powered executive, it is silly to come in with those damn torn jeans. Wear a suit and tie! Other than that, I don't care what anyone is wearing. I used to tell agents who ask what their clients should wear, 'Anything that gets them through the streets without being arrested.' "

Sometimes a casting director may suggest that you dress in a certain way for an audition—obviously, unless you are offended by the directive, do so. Juliet Taylor describes instances in which she might ask an actor to dress in a particular manner for an audition: "We aren't keen on telling actors to dress for parts unless we are really taking a leap and having them come in for something that isn't like them at all. Or if we have an off-beat idea about a character we might ask them to come in, for instance, in a jacket and tie, knowing the actor doesn't generally wear that, or the character doesn't seem like a jacket-and-tie-type guy."

Prepare: Considering how hard it is to find work as an actor, it is surprising to note how many actors show up at auditions unprepared. Don't be one of them. More than any other subject, this one sends directors and casting directors into a tizzy.

Robert Allan Ackerman: "It is disturbing, irritating, and annoying to audition actors who haven't read the script. To me it means they don't want the part. If they don't want the part they shouldn't bother coming in."

Bob Moss: "When you come into a room to audition, I want you to be ready. I don't care if you had a bad day, a bad subway ride, or somebody bumped into you in the street. I'm not interested in any of that. I have auditioned actors who came rushing in after another audition, breathless and having not read the play, and I can assure you I won't audition them again. On the other hand, I recall one actor I auditioned for the play Sleuth who was prepared to play the younger man, the older man, an English accent, and everything else the part required. I didn't cast him, but I never forgot him and I called his agent to say how impressed I was with him. If I have a part for him, I would call him in a second."

Marion Dougherty: "I'll tell you what I hate. I hate when somebody comes in apologizing for not having read the material. If they are not interested enough to do preparation on their own, they should just come in and do the best they can. I am not fond of people who pace around the room and go through this 'getting ready to do the scene' routine. Just sit down and read the best you can and don't apologize for it. I hate apologies."

Be Aware of Your Environment: Theatre auditions take place on stages; film interviews take place in offices. Common sense should tell you how much voice projection is required, or how big your gestures need to be. Alexia Fogel offers this: "The distance that you are playing when you are working with a camera is a much shorter distance than when you are trying to reach the back of a theatre. So play the distance of the room. The space is defined differently, but the acting isn't—film and television doesn't mean smaller acting. In all auditions, you are only expected to suggest something, but you want to suggest it with a fair amount of truth."

Audition Often: Auditioning often is the best way to get used to auditioning and to get good at it. Everyone finds auditioning nerve-racking, but you will be less likely to see the end result as rejection and more likely to see it as part of your work and profession if you do it regularly. With all the variables involved in casting a part, you must understand your talent, or audition, may have nothing to do with your not getting a part. Good advice from B. D. Wong is: "If you want to be an actor, strengthen those parts of you which allow you to cope and survive. You are not going to die because of an audition, so why beat yourself up? If you can overcome the fear of someone laughing at you, then perhaps you will be able to succeed as a professional actor."

Regarding auditioning for roles that you have little chance of winning: This won't come up that often, but if it does, consider how a busy casting director might feel when you arrive for the audition. If there is not a smidgen of hope that you are right for the role, the casting director will probably be annoyed to have his or her time wasted. If you feel a connection to the material and believe something in you will allow you to play the part even if it is a stretch, then go for it. Remember, what counts is your believability as the character, not simply your ability to play the part.

Don't Change Your Interpretation at a Callback: All the casting directors mentioned this as a mistake. If they are calling you back they liked what you did the first time, so stick with it.

Juliet Taylor's advice: "Sometimes an actor comes in and reads for us and we think what they've done is very interesting and we ask them to come back and read for the director. They then come back with an entirely different approach to the part, and we want to die. What they don't understand is we are rooting for them, we want them to come back and be great—it is to our advantage."

Not only should your approach be the same at a callback as it was for the audition, so should your look, unless you are told otherwise. Often a casting director will say "Come back in a dress," or with makeup, or in a suit and tie. Then, and only then, should you change your look.

Have Patience: Time and time again you hear about an actor's getting a job because he or she had impressed someone at another audition. So each time you audition you may actually be auditioning for a part yet to be even written. Jessica Lange auditioned for the role Mary Steenburgen eventually played in the movie *Going South*, but she wasn't offered the part. Her audition, however, so impressed someone who later was working on *The Postman Always Rings Twice* remake that he suggested her for the part and she got it. The editor on that film was so excited by the chemistry between Jessica Lange and Jack Nicholson that he recommended her for the lead in *Frances*, a role for which she eventually received an Academy Award nomination. The moral of the story: From one "failed" audition came two crucial movie roles and one Oscar nomination!

5
Agents and Managers

An actor absolutely cannot survive without an agent in L.A. But in New York you can. —Jim Carnahan, agent

Finding an agent or a manager can become an obsession for many young actors that can be extremely nonproductive. True, an agent or a good manager can get you those elusive auditions and interviews with casting directors you wouldn't be able to get on your own. True, that in Los Angeles your chances of getting an audition without an agent are about nil. But it is also true that you can find work without an agent, and that you should try.

Alexia Fogel, head of prime-time casting for ABC TV, puts it this way: "Most New York casting directors are thorough about young actors and will bring them in even if they don't have an agent." Actor B. D. Wong, who began building his career without an agent, observes, "You do not need an agent to read *Backstage!*"

The point we are making is that to focus all your energy on finding an agent is a misdirected goal, because the best way to attract an agent or manager is to have your work seen—either at a school presentation or in a professional

143

situation. What should you do? Spend a minimum amount
of time contacting agents and a maximum amount of time
training, auditioning, and working. Eventually an agent
will see your work or a casting director will see you and
recommend you to an agent. Remember, the regional and
New York casting community is a very small and talkative
group of people who converse with agents on an almost
daily basis. Few agents would ignore a recommendation
from a casting director who was impressed with your audition or performance; an agent interview can follow.

Does this mean you should not send your picture and
résumé to agents or inform them of upcoming projects?
No, but simply be aware that it is extremely rare for an
agent to invite an actor in for an interview solely because
of a picture and résumé. Of course, there are always exceptions. An agent might be mesmerized by a beautiful
face or impressed with an actor's training. An agent could
have just received a breakdown that he or she cannot find
a submission for among his clients, and you happen to fit
the bill. Or perhaps an agent noticed you perform in a play
once and just needed a little reminder to call you in. For
these possibilities alone it is worthwhile to spend a por-
tion of your time, energy, and money (pictures and postage
are very expensive) pursuing agents, but it is more important to work and study.

It is important to be selective regarding which agents
you contact, because some agencies are not interested in
representing newcomers. The smaller independent agencies in New York (e.g., Strain & Jennett; Bret Adams), especially those that work exclusively with actors, are more
willing to bring in new people than the middle-sized agencies that work with other talents (writers, directors, etc.).
Also, the very large agencies are sometimes willing to take
an unknown talent because they have the staff to develop
them.

Smaller agencies often handle a particular type of client—extremely beautiful, offbeat, ethnic, commercial, etc. And within agencies certain agents handle specific types of clients. For instance, at Paradigm, one agent said he had "a real bent for the unusual, quirky, or unique—actors who can play a wide range of characters," while another agent was interested in young people who are going to be stars—commercial-looking, ingenue types who get cast as the love interest. So be sure to do some homework before blindly sending out your picture and résumé. There are two books that we recommend: *The N.Y. Agent Book* and *The L.A. Agent Book*, both by K. Callen and published by Sweden Press in California.

The biggest complaint budding actors have about agents is that they habitually say "Tell me when you are in something and I'll come to see you." (The second biggest complaint is that they don't come.) The truth is, agents do try to see as much as they can, especially young, aggressive agents who can earn recognition by finding talented unrepresented actors to bring to their agency.

Agents and managers do scour off and off-off-Broadway theatres, Equity Waiver productions, small showcase productions, readings, schools, and television commercials. You might not be aware of them, but they are out there hunting.

It should be noted that it is more important to have representation in Los Angeles for several reasons, one being that in New York the concept of the "open call" exists, where anyone can go to an audition; no such thing exists in Los Angeles—you simply must have an agent to get an audition. Also, the theatre and film community in New York is much smaller than in L.A.; as one manager put it, "New York is a tight little island where everyone knows everyone else and everything that's going on." Los Angeles is more spread out, not only geographically but also activity-wise. Lastly, the stakes are higher in Los Angeles. An actor on an episodic TV series probably earns more in a week than a New York theatre actor earns in a year.

THE DIFFERENCE
BETWEEN AGENTS AND MANAGERS

The primary difference between agents and managers is that agents must be franchised by the unions in order to represent and negotiate for clients, while there is no official sanction for managers, who are never allowed to negotiate on behalf of clients. In other words, anyone can call him or herself a manager, and unfortunately many unqualified people do.

A respected personal manager who handles top-of-the-line talent only told us off the record: "Because personal managers are unlicensed, anybody's mother or dog can say they are someone's manager. I respect maybe three or four [managers]. Every year the agencies—ICM, William Morris, C.A.A., and others—have some assistants who don't make the cut. During the time these assistants are employed by the agencies they talk to the young actors more than the agent does—giving them their appointments, etc.—and become their best friends. So many people who call themselves personal managers today were assistant agents yesterday. They tell young actors that because they've worked at the big agencies they can guide them through it—so more and more often these inexperienced people are becoming personal managers. But even worse are mothers, husbands, and other hanger-oners."

Managers have far fewer clients than agents. A good management office may handle only fifteen or twenty clients and employ three to eight people to service them. An agency, on the other hand, may represent five hundred or more actors, with a much lower ratio of personnel to clients.

Managers are able to charge a larger commission to actors, often 15 percent of what they earn, as opposed to the 10 percent that agents charge.

The basic functions of agents and managers differ. An agent's primary function is to get his or her clients opportunities (i.e., auditions) for employment and negotiate the deal once a job is secured. Managers, at least good ones, function almost as guides or partners in determining the right career moves for their clients. Lois Zetter, president of LeMond/Zetter Management, Inc., a highly respected personal management company in Los Angeles that handles actors with "star potential," offers this: "I sometimes think of myself as a mother tiger protecting a bunch of cubs from the cold, cruel world. And believe me, it is a tough world out here in California. My late partner [Bob LeMond] used to say 'Show business will use you at the lowest level at which you are willing to be used' and I would add that if you work at that level the industry will rarely let you climb up the ladder from there."

Some agents, particularly at smaller agencies, function in both capacities, taking a more active role in guiding an actor's overall career. These people could be classified as agent/managers.

WHO NEEDS A MANAGER?

Not all actors need managers. Each actor's career is distinct and must be evaluated individually, but as a general principle there are two kinds of actors who benefit most from personal management. The first is an actor who is represented by a big, busy agency. The role of the manager has evolved over the past few years as much of the film industry became corporate in both structure and outlook. Long gone are the days when movie studios "nurtured" young discoveries and prepared them for stardom. Personal manager Jim Curtan explains: "The studios and big agencies have a corporate agenda. Our function, as managers, among other things, is to have no agenda other than managing our clients' careers, to make sure that our clients' careers are served every day and don't get lost in the greater need of big corporations." Actress Ally Sheedy, who doesn't feel the need for a personal manager currently, puts it this way: "Because my agent takes a personal interest and she's available to me, I don't feel like I'm one of a thousand clients. But sometimes, in a huge agency, you can get lost in the shuffle—then it is good to have a personal manager."

Agent Jim Carnahan, of Susan Smith Associates in Los Angeles—an agency that doesn't work with many managers—concurs: "It is a fact of life that all agents have their favorite clients—they will read every script the actor gets close to and advise them on minute details. But there are other actors who don't get that attention from an agent. An actor must have someone in his or her life who really believes in them. If you find that in an agent, great; if you find that in a manager, great." Referring to the role of a manager as "that other voice," Carnahan also notes: "If you are very hot, you may want more voices—it depends on what you feel you need. It gets hard sometimes and you need someone to keep you going. But the bottom line is that actors must have agents to negotiate; they don't have to have managers."

The second category of those who might benefit from personal management is young actors without agents who can derive much benefit from the attention of a personal manager. The LeMond/Zetter Agency is known for taking on beginners and working with them prior to and throughout a period of celebrity. For example, John Travolta was discovered at the age of fifteen by the late Bob LeMond in a dinner theatre in New Jersey. Actor Mickey Rourke was sent to the management company by his acting teacher because she felt he had professional potential; LeMond/Zetter agreed, and Rourke spent the first eight years of his career with them.

For the most part, LeMond/Zetter gets their clients through recommendations from agents, casting directors, and acting teachers. But actors have been unearthed by the firm in unlikely ways, too—a hairdresser recommended one client, a bookstore owner recommended another, and Bob LeMond saw the good looks and charisma needed for a leading man in, of all people, his window cleaner—Jon-Erik Hexum, who sadly died in an accident just as his career was taking off.

Ally Sheedy got her career rolling after a personal manager came into her life. Here's what happened:

"I was fifteen when I got my manager and it is unusual how I found her. Because of a book I wrote when I was twelve, I was asked to be on the Mike Douglas talk show. He asked me if I wanted to be a writer when I grew up and I answered, 'No, I'm going to be an actress.' A manager, Breanna Benjamin, who had a small company in New York called For Children Only, saw the program and called my mom's literary agency. My mom told her I wasn't interested and hung up. But then, being the wonderful, honest mom that she is, she told me Breanna called. I went to meet her and she soon had me free-lancing with different agents in the city and auditioning for commercials. I auditioned at least three times a week. I liked it. I did a lot of commercials. It was good that it happened for me that way.

"My manager taught me different things and eventually she got me my first agent. She was always on me about dressing appropriately, which I apparently did not do.

Because I did so many commercials in New York, when I went out to Hollywood I found a commercial agent right away. In New York you can free-lance with different agents, but in Los Angeles you really have to sign with one agent for commercials and another for theatrical work, meaning TV and films. Right away in L.A. I did a Mc-Donald's commercial and then a Pizza Hut one, and I really wanted to find a theatrical agent. My manager came out from New York and called a wonderful agent, Judy Schoen, who was then with Writers and Artists agency. I clicked with her immediately—she was funny and warm and invited me back to do a monologue. The whole agency was there listening to me, and it was terrifying because I didn't know they would all be there. It helped that Judy was right there championing me along. My monologue was Frankie from *The Member of the Wedding*. They said Fine, we are going to sign you."

Actor Gabriel Olds also received his professional start from a personal manager; like Ally, Gabriel's manager found him at an early age—thirteen—on a movie line!
"I've been interested in acting since I was ten years old, so by the time thirteen rolled around I had done four school plays and had enough of an ego to believe I could be a professional actor. So I set out to try to find an agent. I didn't get very far. Then one day I was standing outside a movie theatre when a woman also standing on the line began to talk to me. She said my all-American look would be great for commercials, that I didn't have to be able to act, and that she was a personal manager. I said 'Hey! I can act,' but she didn't believe me. I went to see her in her office and did a monologue. She took me on as a client and recommended I study with Susan Greenhill, a teacher who specialized in training kids. It took three years, but eventually I started learning to act, though I still wasn't

very good at commercials. Susan Greenhill advised me to continue to train and suggested various studios. I ended up going to all of them. I studied with Gloria Maddox at Terry Schreiber Studio, and at Michael Howard Studio I took a Shakespeare class. I was taking three classes a week while I was in high school. Also, I did a couple of off-Broadway and off-off-Broadway plays. Because I was under eighteen I lied about my age to get into these classes—that was the only way I would have been admitted.

"So I owe a lot to my manager, Jean Fox [Fox/Albert Management]. I'm still with her. She sets up appointments like an agent and she's the best negotiator I know—but she can't legally make certain deals for me especially in L.A. She helped me get my first part in a feature film, and now she is helping me find the right agent."

Even beginning actors should examine a manager's credentials to make certain he or she will guide your career with intelligence and integrity. You want a manager who can take you where you want to go, one who is appropriate for the current level of your career and your hopes for the future. Realize also that some actors are able to find agents without the help of a manager. Many graduates from prestigious drama schools are approached by agents early on, and other actors are just as fortunate. Actor B. D. Wong survived nicely in New York without an agent, but realized he needed one in L.A. He went to the Bessie Lou Agency, a small agency that handles Asian actors, and was sent to read for movies and TV. James McDaniel was approached by his first agent while taking dance classes in New York. He got the first job—for a Pepsi commercial—the agent sent him on. He was approached by his current agent after the agent saw him in a play in New York: "I liked him. I could talk to him. I signed with him."

WHAT YOU CAN EXPECT FROM A GOOD MANAGER

The best managers have only one goal—to do what is best for their clients' careers. Every decision is based on this precept. Lesser managers and even some agents might have other motives, such as immediate monetary gain, using one actor to service another, or, at the worst, just being a leech. Personal manager Jim Curtan offers this guideline: "The thing an actor should look for in a personal manager is passion. Because we are involved on a personal level with our clients every day, there has to be a connection. Everyone in this town [L.A.] is good at courtship, and very few of us are good at marriage. As soon as you've conquered, you move on to the next conquest. But we make marriages with our clients and an actor has the right to expect that. Lois Zetter says, "With regard to what to be wary of, contracts longer than three years, commissions higher than fifteen percent, a manager telling you to expect a lot of charges to be levied upon you, and excessive hype—'By Thursday I'll have you riding in a limo with the president of Paramount'—because that is pretty unlikely when you're a young sprat. Also, beware of a contract that doesn't give you, the actor, the final say as to whether you say yes or no to a job."

Although everyone agrees that at the start of a career it is a good idea to work no matter what the job, in fact there are jobs that certain young actors should not take. A clever personal manager will steer you away from these. Personal manager Jim Curtan explains: "In the old days, if an actor was in a real clinker but was under a contract, the studio had an investment and would fix the damage. Also, actors used to work much more—today even our biggest stars only do one or two movies a year. What is scary today is that a gifted actor out of Juilliard might decide to do a martial arts picture just to pay the rent and then find it difficult to be perceived as anything other than a martial arts–type actor. It is very hard to change the audience's perception of you today. This is one reason it is important for an actor to be guided from the beginning of a career."

Lois Zetter adds, "If a client has to take off his clothes and roll around in mud to be in a film, we say that's not going to get him anywhere. We are much more oriented [than agents] to advise our clients to say no to things that can be destructive for them."

A similar problem, and one that is more likely to arise in Los Angeles than in New York, is making the transition from television or New York stage to film. Here again, a wise personal manager can offer direction.

Lois Zetter: "There are television roles that can make an actor a star and make him lots of money, but ultimately ruin his career. When we look for television series for our clients we are careful about more than the quality of writing. We consider if, should the series become a hit, the part will help the actor get to the next step and not leave him behind in the land of lost TV stars. A good manager looks to the future."

A conflict of interest, with regard to television work, can develop between actors and agents—especially when the agent is with a small agency that survives on commissions from their clients' low-maintenance, steady-income TV jobs. Such agents are more apt to recommend that an actor take TV work rather than hold out for a film. It is interesting to note that even if the actor is wooed away by another agency, the original agency still gets commissions for the life of the series. These and other conflicts of interest could be the reason actors leave their agents more frequently than they leave their managers. (Another could be that all agents' contracts have a ninety-day out clause. Most manager contracts are for at least three years.)

Personal managers should also provide actors with often needed objectivity. Lois Zetter again: "Actors are by definition subjective and don't look at the larger picture, so an actor might read a script and only see that there is a great role in it to play. Actors tend not to look at the larger picture. They also think they can fix what is wrong in a role or a script, just through their acting abilities. When we evaluate work, we look for an even exchange, that is that the material our client is asked to do is worthy of the talent our client offers. We make certain an actor is not just being used by the material to make awful stuff tolerable, but rather is challenged and rewarded."

Good personal managers are collaborators, working with actors to build their careers and bringing them to the point where they have career choices to make. Again, it must be said that good agents are also comrades in arms, but often they are too busy or too business-minded to function as such. Personal manager Jim Curtan: "In the early days of management, some agencies weren't interested in working with personal managers, but the dynamics of the business has changed and some agents prefer their clients have a manager to back them up; in fact, the major agencies are more likely to take a young client if he or she has a manager.

Lois Zetter adds: "The agent wants a client to have a marketing package—the correct picture, the correct tape —but most don't have the time to guide them. What we do is groom our clients to be ready to go to an audition. We help them select the right acting teacher, we help them put together a demo tape. We give them guidance as to what a casting director might be looking for in an interview and ideas of how to mend what's wrong. For instance we might suggest that their goal in an interview is to make the casting director comfortable rather than 'I must get this job,' which will be seen as desperation. An agent doesn't have the time to sit down with an actor and tell him how to behave at an audition or interview."

Jim Curtan adds: "We also take the time to get detailed feedback from casting directors about our clients' auditions. For episodic television this isn't possible, but for a movie or a play we take the time to make our clients understand what the feedback means so the next time they audition they can better their chance. One of the most important things a good manager can do for an actor is set them up with a powerful agent. Generally, the more powerful the manager, the more powerful their agent contacts.

As Lois Zetter explains: "We work with the bigger and more established agencies, so an actor with very few credits might even be able to get in to meet a bigger agent than he might have on his own because of our connections and reputation. We give the 'Good Housekeeping Seal of Approval' when we send an actor in—it is saying we see and believe in something here, and agents know we have a good track record."

With more and more stars parlaying their acting success into power and the ability to generate projects, personal managers are taking on a new function in the 1990s. Jim Curtan says, "What actors have to think about today that they never had to think about before is how to be entrepreneurial. There was a time when you could be passive and pampered as an actor and expect everything to be taken care of for you. That doesn't work anymore, besides the fact that the system destroyed the lives of a lot of people. Actors, at least the ones we are interested in working with, must be willing to take responsibility, to show people how to use them—that is where our collaborative part comes in. What makes it exciting for personal managers like us is when someone is interested in building a career that stretches them as artists—to do as Kevin Costner did once he was discovered, which was to develop his own projects. Ideally, actors should have as much autonomy as possible. Sadly, today talent is looked at as a product. The business is being run by people coming out of Wharton School of Business instead of people with a love of show business; and many of them don't understand what actors do. It is up to the actor to show what they can do. Good managers are collaborators with actors in this endeavor—we let them know how they are being perceived and received, because they can't always tell. Our job is to help our clients make their talents irresistible to the buyer."

Integrity, credentials, background, wisdom, sound judgment, connections, and enterprise are what a good manager should provide. Unfortunately, many do not. So if you are approached by a manager, make sure to do your homework, that is, find out who his or her clients are, which agents he or she has relationships with, and how he or she perceives your future.

WHAT MANAGERS LOOK FOR IN ACTORS

Again, depending on their influence and style, and whether they are based in New York or Los Angeles, personal managers differ in what they look for in potential clients. At the top level in Los Angeles for instance, personal managers tend to be interested in actors with movie-star potential. Lois Zetter, whose agency is known for managing actors with leading-role potential, is very specific about her standards. "Our criteria are talent, marketable looks, and charisma. If an actor has two of those things, they can get jobs. But to be a star, you need all three of those things." Marketable looks is an interesting and ever-changing standard. Actors like Danny DeVito or Bette Midler both have marketable looks in today's market and are certainly stars, yet in years past they probably would have been considered character actors.

■

Jim Curtan's test for prospective clients is the degree of aspiration they manifest: "The client has to want it as much as we want it for him. One of the most exhausting things in the world for a manager to deal with is an actor's ambivalence. When you are working with a small list of clients, they all have to be out there striving."

Both personal managers agree they look for actors with long-term commitment—actors who know what kind of career they want, rather than those who just want a job. If they believe an actor can attain the kind of career he or she claims to want, and if they can serve such a career, the result is a contract.

WHAT YOU CAN EXPECT
FROM A GOOD AGENT

Agents have two responsibilities: to get auditions for the actors they represent and to negotiate the best possible deal for the client when a job offer is made. A good agent is aggressively well informed and tenacious about getting his clients considered for roles he believes they can do—even when initial interest is nil. Even more important than the connections, more important than the prestige of the agency, is that the agent believes in and appreciates an actor's talent. If you do not receive that value from your agent, he will not be effective for you, no matter how great an agent he might be or how powerful his agency is considered.

Agent Ed Betz, who has worked at the William Morris agency, the Lantz Office, and at APA, explains: "It doesn't really matter what agency represents you in the beginning; it's how the agent feels about you. It takes a lot of work on the part of the agent in the beginning—a lot of phoning around, et cetera, and there's very little in it for the agent, little money to be made, really. If you find an agent willing to commit to you, it doesn't matter what the agency."

Another New York agent agrees: "Find an agent who loves you and believes in you and will fight for you, rather than one who is powerful, because being with CAA or William Morris and not going on auditions doesn't help."

Faith and advocacy are important qualities to look for in an agent. But so is power—and in show business, information is power. A well-meaning agent who is the last to know what's happening is not likely to further your career. One of the benefits of large, powerful agencies is that they tend to employ the sharpest, most well-informed people, and so at least you are ensured of being at the center of things. This is particularly true in Los Angeles, where most film and TV projects are generated, and a well-connected agent can learn about upcoming projects very early on from producers, studio development executives, and casting people. Also, large agencies handle major writers, directors, and producers and like to package projects with their own clients when possible.

There is a more formal way for agents to learn about who is casting what roles than show business gossip and sneak previews of scripts: through something called a breakdown service. Breakdowns can only be obtained by franchised talent agencies working out of commercial space. A good agent scours and scrutinizes the breakdowns daily. Essentially, a breakdown is a description of a film or play and the cast of characters required. Most casting directors working in film, television, and theatre utilize a breakdown service. The casting director submits a description of the roles, says who the director is, and when the project is coming to town (breakdowns are used both in New York and Los Angeles), and the breakdown service sends out the information immediately to all agents who subscribe to the service. One agent refers to breakdowns as "the Help Wanted for actors."

But merely reading the breakdowns and submitting pictures and résumés of clients does not always ensure an audition. Sometimes persuading and cajoling a casting director is necessary, and that is what a good agent does.

Jim Carnahan, an agent with the Los Angeles branch of Susan Smith Associates: "As an agent, there are times you write a name down on a piece of paper and you know any agent would have thought to put this name down and any casting director would have thought to bring this actor in and any director in his right mind would hire him. But there are other times when you know your fighting helped someone get the job, and that's the exciting part for an agent. Ultimately, talent gets an actor a job, but sometimes it takes knocking down some walls to get an actor in the room. There have been times when I got an actor an audition by changing minds or staying on top of a project because I so believed in the actor's talent. I once put a twenty-seven-year-old Irish man up for a lead in which he had to play a seventeen-year-old Jewish boy. I stayed on top and kept saying 'This actor is wonderful; you must see him even if physically he's not what you're looking for.' After they saw seven hundred and fifty actors, they brought him in and he got the part. Those are the times that you're proud of your work as an agent."

In addition to being a champion of your talent and alert to prospective auditions, a good agent is one you can trust, which is often best judged by a "gut" reaction to the agent. There are nightmare stories told about agents who sign actors to protect their existing clients from direct competition with an actor very similar in type. The new actor is rarely sent out on auditions. Less contemptible, though certainly no less destructive, are agents who lie about why you didn't get a job.

Stephen Hirsh, an agent with Paradigm, considers trust between actor and agent crucial to a working relationship: "Because we place so much faith in the people we represent and give them so much support, trust develops, but it's a building process. Because of that trust we can be frank and honest with clients, even when it hurts. I don't mean we say 'You lost it because you were terrible'—we cushion the fall but try to give honest feedback from the casting director. Without trust we couldn't do that."

A New York agent offers this: "If you don't get a job, ask your agent why. It's an agent's job to find out and tell you why, or else he's not doing his job."

Jim Carnahan also affirms that actors should expect honesty from an agent. "As an agent you want the actor to trust you, to trust that you are making decisions appropriately and will guide you the way you wish to be guided. That is why I tell actors to go with your gut, go with the person you want to spend the next ten or even twenty years of your life with and who you trust. It is very much like getting married. I mean, agents really do hold actors' careers in their hands, so you have to trust and care about each other. When it comes to choosing an agent, at a certain level we are all the same—we can all get you on this movie or that movie, so go with the one who makes you feel comfortable."

Agent Ed Betz supports the idea that a trustworthy, dutiful agent always gives an actor honest feedback: "I am honest with my clients all the time. I tell them when they've blown an audition. I get angry when they are late for an audition—that is unforgivable, I don't care who you are.

I have no patience for meshugas, like not wanting to cut your hair for a role, and I say so. I believe in nurturing talent, and part of that is being honest."

Jim Carnahan makes another good point relevant to appraising an agent: "People want different things out of an agent. There are some people who want someone who can read and evaluate material—agents who represent them on an intellectual basis. There are others who want an agent who is a hardball, tough negotiator. You should go with what you feel secure with, or else you'll be fighting all along the way."

Actress Jane Adams left her first agent for just that reason: the agent suggested Jane leave Juilliard and take a part on a sitcom, a recommendation she couldn't live with. "I got my first agent after I did a play at Playwrights Horizons. Actually, one of the agents from the agency [Harry Abrams, Inc.] came to see the play—which by the way wasn't a success—but didn't like me—he thought I was too plump. A week later the head of the agency came, and after the show he gave me his card and asked me to come in. Suddenly I had representation and it felt great because I was being sent out on all these auditions. Then I was offered a role on a series and I got a lot of pressure to take it. I didn't want to leave Juilliard, which I would have had to do, so I decided not to take the role. I was made to feel like I was in the wrong and I thought, Wait—clearly there is something wrong with this relationship. Right at that time I was doing a play at the O'Neill summer theatre and a friend introduced me to an agent at J. Michael Bloom. So I switched. They were great, but when I went out to L.A. I felt I wanted to be with an agency that handled more directors and so I went with ICM and loved it. Everyone says at a large agency you have to be careful because you

can get lost. Well, you just have to know what you want.
I would know something was wrong if suddenly I wasn't
being seen for all these things. Agents aren't going to make
your career—you have to do that. They can get me the
auditions, but I have to go in and get the job."

Regardless of what is most important to you in an agent,
certainly a good agent should be a smart, strong, and gutsy
negotiator, because it is the agent's job to arrange your
salary, schedule, and any perks that might be available.

To sum up what you can expect from a good agent:
someone who believes in your talent, is willing to go out
on a limb for you, is well informed, gets you in as many
audition doors as possible, gives you honest feedback, is
trustworthy, and negotiates a good contract. What he or
she can't do is get you jobs. That is up to you.

WHAT AGENTS LOOK FOR IN ACTORS

Agents want to represent actors who will make money for
their agency—sooner or later. The more assurance they
have that this will happen, the more likely they will be
to sign you. In the case of unproved talent, agents have
several measurements, including an actor's training, demeanor, looks, desire to succeed, and apparent talent, but
ultimately it comes down to a gut reaction. Listen to agent
Ed Betz describe why he signed a particular young client:
"I took one look at him and boom—something—it was a
hunch and I signed him."

Stephen Hirsh, New York agent, describes "a certain
something, a gleam in the eye" as a motivating factor for
signing a client. Another agent who handles several actors
who sing, says: "When people come in to sing for me, if
they give me the chills I consider working with them; if I
feel they'll pay attention, listen to me, and can accept who

they are, I'll sign them." In other words, the process is subjective, discretionary, and speculative. And with new talent, which requires much time, energy, and money on the part of the agent before any benefits are accrued, the selection of clients has high stakes. This is why agents consider an actor's *training* before signing him or her, to make the choice less of a gamble.

Ed Betz again: "I think a Juilliard credit on the résumé is a foot in the door. I am impressed by it. I know how difficult it is to get accepted into that program and how good the training is. Classical training gives the actor discipline and a confidence and an intelligent approach to the material; they know how to read and how to find the character. Yale, SUNY-Purchase, and North Carolina School of the Arts impress me. But a Juilliard credit is a very nice label and the most impressive."

Joanna Colonna, an agent with Paradigm in Los Angeles, agrees: "I like actors who have come out of the good schools because they have well-rounded training. They know how to do Shakespeare, they know how to sing, they know stage combat and dialects, and so on."

Stephen Hirsh adds: "Actors who come out of good schools are more easily prepared to make choices for various roles. You can throw out a script and a part to a trained actor and you know he can create the persona. Acting is developing a character, and when an actor is in front of a casting director, he must make choices, because making choices is what it is all about. We feel people coming out of good training schools—like Juilliard, Yale, Purchase, Boston University, NYU, Carnegie Mellon, North Carolina—have the best resources to make those choices. I'm not saying that's the only way to learn—I've seen very good actors who haven't been through a training program—but it's a plus if they have."

Jim Carnahan admits some of his favorite actors of another generation got their training in theatre as opposed to a conservatory, but agrees today there is something to be said about the kind of training you get from a top drama school: "A lot of our actors [from Susan Smith Associates] come from Yale and Juilliard. So, yes, it does make a difference if you went to Yale or Juilliard. The reason is theatre. It makes a big difference if you've been trained in theatre. And drama school is a good place to get theatre training. It means you've worked on important material with good actors and directors. That's the bottom line— theatre training."

Besides training, agents look for other signs that suggest an actor will be a good investment for the agency.

Stephen Hirsh: "One thing I look for in an actor is that he or she is as motivated as I am. I'm aggressive, young, and really going for it because I'm hungry. I like to see actors with the same attitude. In other words, I want to hear them say they want to work *and* they want to work on their craft. Actors worry me who just say 'I want to work in movies.' I love to hear an actor say they will give one hundred percent to their art—because I'm giving a hundred and fifty percent to their career. And giving one hundred percent means following up auditions with post-cards and thank-you notes—to make sure people know who they are; working showcase productions even without pay to help an agent present them; listening to criticism and working on improving their auditions; staying in class; listening to the grapevine and reporting back to the agent; and generally not leaving it all to chance, or the wind, or the agent."

Joanna Colonna says one thing she takes into consideration when determining whether a client is right for her is if the actor's expectations for him or herself are in sync with the agency's expectations. "If, after a one-on-one interview with an actor, there is interest, we'll ask them to come back to do a scene or a monologue and meet the rest of the agency. One specific thing we take into consideration is if their dreams match our dreams. And does the actor have a sense of reality about himself."

Stephen Hirsh tells about a young actor who got in for an interview but ultimately was not signed by the agency because his notion of himself differed entirely from the agent's observations: "I had an actor in here the other day who said he could be going up for all of Tom Cruise's roles. I didn't agree with him, and I knew right away that he didn't have a realistic perception of who he was if he thought he was going up for leading-man roles. During an interview I always ask questions that tell me if an actor has a sense of reality about himself—like which actors he relates to, are there actors whose careers he would like to emulate. I can tell where they are going and if we are going to jibe."

THE AGENT INTERVIEW

Once an agent's interest in you is sparked (by a photo and résumé, or in L.A. by your tape, by seeing you at a school presentation or in a play or commercial, or through a recommendation), his or her next move is usually to invite you in for an interview. If the first interview goes well, you will possibly be invited back to meet and perhaps audition for other agents within the agency.

*Joanna Colonna, who began her agenting career dis-
covering new young talent, is most forthcoming about
what agents look for during the interview process:* "There
are so many qualities I look for. When they first walk in
I want to see a realness about them—that there is a real
person here, not just an actor speaking from behind a wall.
So many actors program themselves beforehand as to what
to say, and yet spontaneity and the ability to think on your
feet is so important in this business. It's the same attribute
that attracts you to a person in real life—we've all met
people who are boring and one-dimensional and others
who have a really great imagination and persona. I hate it
when actors can't converse during the interview and are
afraid to ask questions. The worst interviews are when I
ask all the questions and an actor just answers."

*Stephen Hirsh, because he works for an agency that does
sign new talent, will sometimes call an actor in for an
interview based on his or her photo and résumé. He re-
states Joanna Colonna's watchfulness:* "We like to see if
an actor is a quick thinker because we send a lot of people
out for generals to meet casting directors and directors,
and we want to see how they will do. So we try to get
them to talk by asking questions like why they want to
act, or tell me something about yourself that isn't on your
résumé. Not many actors do well in general interviews."

If you pass muster in the interview process, most agents
will then ask you to audition for them.

*Joanna Colonna reviews what happens after a prom-
ising interview:* "Then we have to see their work. Because
a lot of young actors don't have many credits, I have them
do a scene here in the office. I give them a scene, they
go home to work on it and then come back. This reveals
so much—because young people—especially those not

aware of the camera—mumble, move around too much, have accents they need to work on. There are many things to look at: attitude, looks, versatility, and of course they need to be able to act—to bare their souls in order to create different personas. And I try to determine how hard they are willing to work. Stars are made, but it can take years. Look at Alec Baldwin—he was in New York for ten years before his career started rocketing."

We have already heard casting directors and directors stress the importance of walking in the door of an audition confidently; the same holds true for interviews with agents:

Ed Betz: "You've got to come in with an attractive frame of mind—in a personable way, with energy and charisma. I've had actors schlep their way in here and you think, I don't want to be with this person. I work very closely with and spend a lot of time with my clients—it's almost like adopting children—so if the person comes in here and is not alert and bright and fresh, it is never going to happen. Also, I like actors who like to work. With new talent you sometimes—but not often—hear they will only do certain things. That's just too limiting. If I hear that in an interview, I wouldn't get involved."

An agent interview in L.A. differs somewhat from an agent interview in New York, mainly because agents in Los Angeles usually don't conduct live auditions in their offices. They expect an actor to have a reel or tape and only invite actors in after viewing this compilation of TV and film work.

L.A. agent Jim Carnahan clarifies: "Out here, most actors who get interviews with agents already have some sort of a body of work. Even the twenty-two-year-olds have done at least an MOW, so they have something to show us. In New York agents find prospective clients in plays, or they'll ask an actor to do a live audition in an office; we look at tapes. It makes sense in that that's what we do out here—we put people in TV or film, so that is what we need to see."

There are exceptions to the rule. Jim Carnahan tells about a young actress without any credits, let alone a tape, who his agency auditioned: "A young actress was recommended to us through casting people. She was just off the boat, not even from Juilliard or Yale or one of the schools with a drama program, but from Sarah Lawrence. We did watch her do a few scenes and signed her, but she was an unusual case. On her third professional audition she landed a major role in a network TV series. This is a very rare case."

The best advice we can give you with regard to an agent interview is probably the hardest to follow: Be yourself. Put yourself in the best frame of mind you can and consider the agent's feelings as well. Most agents want you to be likable, talented, and great looking, especially agents who have invited you in for an interview. While there are some mean-spirited agents, as there are mean-spirited people in every profession, most agents don't enjoy saying no any more than you enjoy hearing it. In Jim Carnahan's words: "Being an actor is hard—it is really hard. You spend most of your life being told no. But you know what? I find the hardest part of being an agent is that I spend most of my time giving bad news. Ninety percent of my time is saying, No, you didn't get the part, and here's the reasons why. That's pretty hard, too."

Eventually every actor needs an agent, as much to have someone on his professional side as to get auditions and negotiate contracts. Some actors are lucky and get positive responses from agents they send their pictures and résumés to. Most actors, however, acquire an agent through their work—be it a school presentation, an audition with a casting person, or a reading, showcase, or produced play. So yes, it is important to be represented, but in the beginning your career doesn't depend on your having an agent. And once you are signed by an agent, your career isn't made—you still have to audition and get the jobs. And you still need to maintain control over your career, because no matter how good an agent or manager is, he or she has his own agenda to consider.

Note what Ally Sheedy says about a lesson she wished she had learned earlier in her career: "In the beginning, when I just started to get successful, I wish I had been more careful about advice I received and about people's motives around me. I would have asked more questions and listened more and thought more about whether this is something I should be doing instead of saying, I have to do this part because they want me for it. Agents and managers want to make money, but an actor isn't obliged to do a part just because someone wants you to. I trusted some people I ought not to have."

AGENCY AGREEMENTS

An agent, or artists' manager as he or she is frequently referred to in contracts, as defined by the Screen Actor's Guild, is "a person, co-partnership, association, firm or corporation who or which offers to or does represent, act as representative of, negotiate for, procure employment for, counsel or advise" an actor in connection with or relating to his or her employment or his professional career in general.

Like any other employment agency, the agent must apply to the state labor commission for a license to practice—to solicit work for clients and take a commission from their earnings. The agent or agency must also be franchised: each of the unions (SAG, AFTRA, Equity, AGVA) will grant a qualified agent a franchise that permits the agent to represent performers in that union. (Don't have anything to do with an agent if he or she is not franchised. The unions provide lists of their franchised agents.) The agent, in turn, is required to use the agency contract approved by the union. This restriction is for the protection of the actor because it ensures that an agent cannot represent an actor for terms that are less favorable than those that have been union-approved.

An artist's manager or agency contract, as defined by SAG, is "a contract between an agent and a client providing for the rendering of agency services." The SAG, AFTRA, Equity, and AGVA contracts are all fundamentally the same. Each provides that the actor employs the agent to represent him exclusively in a specific area of the business—legitimate theatre, film, television, etc. The contract specifies the length of the agreement and the commission that the actor agrees to pay the agent, and states that as long as the agent receives commissions from the actor, the agent shall be obliged to "serve" the actor. The first exclusive-management contract an actor signs with an agent will usually be for a period of one year; after that, the usual term of the contract is three years. Of course, in Los Angeles you sign with one agent on an exclusive basis, whereas in New York many actors free-lance, especially early on.

Here are some of the highlights of the details of an agent/actor contract describing the role of the agent:

1. Use all reasonable efforts to assist the actor in procuring employment as an actor.
2. Counsel and advise the actor in matters that concern the professional interests of the actor.

3. The agent will be truthful in his statements to the actor.

4. The agent will not conceal facts from the actor that are pertinent and that the actor is entitled to know.

5. The agent will not engage in dishonest and fraudulent practices with regard to the making or entering into of the agency contract or the performance thereof.

6. The agent's relationship will be that of a fiduciary.

7. The agent, when instructed in writing by the actor not to give out information with reference to the actor's affairs, shall not disclose such information.

8. The agent may represent actors of the same general qualifications and eligibility for the same parts or roles. The agent agrees that, prior to the execution of the agency contract, he will deliver to the actor on request a list of the actors represented by the agent.

9. The agent shall consider only the interests of the actor in any dealings for the actor.

10. The agent is equipped and shall continue to be equipped to represent the interests of the actor ably and diligently.

11. The agent shall seek and confer with producers and others who may employ or recommend employment of the actor, and read scripts made available to him by the actor.

12. At the written request of the actor, the agent shall give the actor information in writing stating what efforts the agent has rendered on behalf of the actor.

13. The agent shall make no binding commitments without the actor's approval.

14. The agent will not execute a contract for the actor at less than union minimum.

6

Tools of the Profession

*We try to be conscientious about going through
unsolicited pictures, but sometimes when you are busy
that's impossible. We divide the pictures into different
categories. If someone has a wonderful face we'll put
them in a "wonderful look" category because we do a
lot of movies that require that kind of face. If they have
a really interesting résumé combined with an interesting
look, we put the picture aside in a general category that
we look through during slow periods and keep referring
back to at a time when we're looking for something
particular.*
—Juliet Taylor

There are certain, important basic tools that every actor
must have in order to effectively go about the business of
being an actor. Without them, you don't exist.

PHOTOGRAPHS
An eight-by-ten black-and-white head shot is a basic requirement of the business. Professional preference currently seems to be for a full-face photograph, done in a
semimatte rather than glossy finish. Along with your ré-

sumé, your photograph is your passport to future possibilities. It will often be the first step in bringing yourself
to the attention of a potential employer and get you in the
door to get the job. You will present your photos at open
calls and mail them out to agents, casting directors, producers, and managers. It's your first line of attack, your
first step in introducing yourself to the people on the other
side of the desk. It is important to have a picture that will
work for you, not against you. It is important to remember
that you are in a business that requires you to sell yourself.
You are the product, and the market is flooded. So you
must not be vague or hesitant about what it is you are
selling, and why it—meaning you—is unique, intriguing,
different. But aim for a realistic, natural photograph that
looks like you.

Here are some telling comments about photographs
from people who look at hundreds of them every day:

Daniel Swee: "A photograph should look as much like the
actor as possible. I don't like pictures that are overly made-
up and overly lit because they don't look like the person.
The actor becomes a generic type instead of a unique individual. All the character is airbrushed out of them. It's
nice when there is actually something going on in someone's expression, when something is happening."

Marion Dougherty: "Many people get pictures that don't
look like them, which is a mistake. They should try to get
a simple head shot that looks just like them. When I interview someone who looks completely different than his
or her photograph, I take a Polaroid and clip it onto the
picture. Sometimes the difference is amazing."

Juliet Taylor: "We prefer straight head shots. Very artistic
shots in which you can't really tell what the person looks

like are irritating and often end up in the wastepaper basket."

Finding the right photographer will take some careful research and a substantial investment, anywhere from $150 to $700 (not including stationery for cover letters, envelopes, and stamps), but if you get one fabulous photograph out of it the expense will be worth it. We suggest you do some serious comparison shopping. Get the names of several different photographers (three or four should do it) from fellow actors whose pictures you like, or ask the advice of your teachers. Take a look at photographers' work and talk with them to find out how they work and how comfortable you feel: can you relax, can you be yourself? And find out what you will be getting for your money.

Jane Adams: "You have to have a great photograph. Mine were expensive, but they were worth the investment."

Many young actors feel they have to spend a fortune on a composite, a group of pictures showing them in every guise imaginable. And some commercial photographers will try to convince an actor that he or she needs a wide array of pictures illustrating his or her different "looks." Don't be fooled. A composite is a waste of money and time unless you are going to do commercials. Basically one good head shot (or two, if you are lucky enough to get two good ones) is what you need. Most photographers will take from sixty to eighty shots in a session and print them up on contact sheets from which you can choose the best one. When you get this contact sheet, if you are having trouble deciding, get some other opinions—from your friends, your enemies, and professionals—before making up your mind. Remember: Choose a photograph that looks like you (at your best, of course).

Your next step will be to have copies made of your picture by a photo service. We suggest starting with an initial batch of 100 photographs. Some of these duplicating services will also print your name and phone number on the front of your photograph if you wish.

RÉSUMÉS

Now that you have your picture, turn it over. Carefully stapled or glued to the back of your eight-by-ten head shot will be your résumé, the other essential tool of the business. Getting a résumé together is a lot easier than getting a good picture, and you will need one, just as much as you need those pictures. They go together.

If you have nothing to put on your résumé at all, other than a high school production of *As You Like It*, you have two alternatives: you can tell the truth, or you can concoct a feasible résumé of parts in plays you *could* have done that are representative of you, that are close to you as a type. Most people we talked with, however, strongly advised against presenting anything but the truth on an actor's résumé. The whole point about these professional autobiographies is that unless you can truthfully say that you had a part in a play or a movie that the people on the other side of the desk have heard about or know about, your white lies about plays and student films aren't going to matter much anyway. And they might come back to haunt you.

If you have few credits, one casting director suggested writing a paragraph that is the absolute truth: "I have been in New York for a year. I acted in high school and college. I've studied with so-and-so and am now studying with so-and-so. I was in a student film. Please see me."

How to Prepare a Résumé

The following information should appear on your résumé. If you are looking for work in New York you will want to list your stage credits first. If you are in Los Angeles, you will probably want to list film and television first, or have two versions of your résumé, depending upon who is getting it. The information contained in your résumé should be neatly laid out on one page, accurately typed, and easy to read. (There are services that specialize in doing résumés and cover letters—for example, Shakespeare Theatrical Mailing Service in New York.)

Name:

Height:

Weight:

Hair Color:

Eye Color:

Service/Machine:

Agent and Agent's Phone Number:
(or Personal Manager and phone number)

Union Affiliations:

Theatre: This section should list the theatre category (Broadway, off-Broadway, regional theatre, etc.), the name of the play, and the part you played in the production, and the name of the director if significant. If you only have college credits, list those.

Film: The name of the film, your role, the director if significant, and the company.

Television: This can be broken up into categories, with the more impressive first—like a movie of the week or a miniseries—then list episodic, then daytime (soaps).

Commercials: Do not list commercials you have done here. Rather, state "Commercials upon request." That is, if you have done any. If not, omit this category.

Training: This is very important, especially when you are starting out and have few credits. Some casting directors suggest putting this training at the top of a résumé, especially if the school is a prestigious one. Include ongoing training that you are involved in, coaches you are working with, and acting classes you are taking with well-known teachers or in well-known techniques like the Meisner Technique.

Special Skills and Abilities: A variety of things can be listed here, such as musical instruments you play, languages you speak, sports you play well—for example, ice skating, swimming, tennis, golf, horseback riding. Also list other abilities and talents you have that may be attractive, offbeat, eye-catching without being silly. You never know what will get you a job. Roller skating, roller blading, juggling? Even driving a car. For extra work include wardrobe.

Once you have picture and résumé together, keep them current and don't show up without them. Nothing seems to annoy agents and casting directors more than an actor who arrives without these vital pieces of equipment.

POSTCARDS AND FLYERS

Postcards printed with your picture on them or flyers can be good devices for reminders, invitations, and follow-ups to agents and casting directors. Janet Foster, casting director: "I remember seeing an actor in the League presentations, thinking she was odd and interesting. She didn't come to New York afterwards or get herself an agent; she disappeared. But a year and a half later she sent me a postcard saying I had asked for her picture and résumé at the Leagues. I said 'Oh, here she is,' and I brought her in for a general audition and then a specific audition. She now has an agent and is doing very well. Her follow-up postcard did the trick."

But don't overdo it. An actor who sends out postcards to agents or casting directors every month to remind them of his or her existence can be irritating, and this strategy is counterproductive if overdone. As Juliet Taylor commented: "There are some people who think that if you can be active enough in the business, you almost don't have to be an actor. We had this young woman in here the other day telling us she had just done a huge mailing of five hundred postcards and that she was willing to work, work, work to get her name around, and in our heads we are saying, Great, but can you act?" Send postcards out when you have a good reason to do so—for example, you are appearing in a terrific showcase, or a commercial is airing, or even if you are going to be going out of town doing something. Interested agents and casting directors will want to keep track of you.

LABELS
There are services that will print up your mailing list on computerized, peel-off mailing labels. Some even do personalized mailings for you to agents, casting directors, producers, and managers.

VIDEOTAPES
Videotapes are not a necessity in New York. However, in Los Angeles, many of the people you will want to be dealing with will want tapes, especially agents who will be the first line of contact you will be attempting to make in that city. Jim Carnahan explains: "We look at tapes out here. It is one of the big differences between New York and L.A. In New York people will tend to come in and do scenes in an office, or an agent will go see them in a play.

What tends to happen out here is people edit together scenes that they have done in a TV show or film and put together what's known as a reel or tape. There is a huge business out here composed of services like Jan's Video that do nothing but record things off television for actors to put on their tapes."

However, realistically, it is difficult, although not impossible, to put together a decent-looking videotape if you haven't yet done anything on film! You will have to carefully prepare a monologue or a scene and find a video production house to tape it. It will be expensive, and chances are it is not likely to impress the people you want to impress, although your mother might like it. However, once you have done some work that can be put on a videotape, for example commercials in which you have speaking parts, or a speaking part in a soap opera, or even a good part in a student film, it can be an extremely useful tool for getting attention.

A collection of your clips should be put on to a professional-quality master tape (¾ inch) from which ½-inch standard VHS copies can be made. The tape should not be longer than eight to ten minutes.

ANSWERING MACHINE/ANSWERING SERVICE

It is important to make yourself readily available to those people in the business who will want to get in touch with you. Either sign up with a reliable answering service or invest in a good answering machine that allows you to call in from wherever you are and get your messages. There are several very good services that specialize in performers and offer twenty-four-hour-a-day service, wake-up calls, tracing, and call forwarding. If you use an answering machine, keep your taped message short and to the point. Don't try to be cute or clever. You'll only annoy your callers. The telephone is an incredibly important means of communication in this business, and it is essential for you that "someone" is always home.

NETWORKING

Finally, don't overlook one of the most important resources that an actor can have. This business is about people and about information and about people talking to people and passing on pieces of information. This process has come to be known as networking. You could call it gossip, or you could call it contacts. Don't neglect this aspect of your business. Keep your ears open. And follow up leads. You may be surprised at what a rich resource other people in your profession can be.

RESOURCES

Faithfully read the trade papers every week. They will be a major source of casting information, although in Los Angeles the most up-to-date news is "published" on the grapevine, and usually only agents have the most recent inside track to what is happening.

Backstage (New York, weekly)
Drama-Logue (Los Angeles, weekly)
The Hollywood Reporter (daily)
Daily Variety
Variety (weekly)
Ross Reports Television (casting, scripts, and production. Long Island City, NY)
Television Index, Inc. (published monthly and widely available in bookstores)

Another source of information is bulletin boards: at the union offices, at your acting school, at the Drama Book Shop on Seventh Avenue in New York or the Samuel

French bookstore on Sunset Boulevard in Los Angeles. You can give them the once-over as you make your rounds for casting notices and other information. It is important that you keep your fingers on these more informal networks of communication.

7

Union Membership

You can't get a union job
unless you're in the union.
And you can't get into the union
without a union job . . .

—Old Saw

And so on. Every actor knows this song because every actor has faced or will face this Kafkaesque situation at a certain point in his or her career. A certain rite of passage, it looms ahead like a brick wall that you will bang up against at least once. A glance through the casting section of *Backstage* or *Show Business* or *Variety* tells you why: many of the casting notices call for Equity or SAG members only. But look again. *Backstage* (New York) and *Drama-Logue* (L.A.) also list lots of casting calls for non-union actors for student films.

Actors who haven't yet managed to join a union resent the fact that the unions make it so difficult to join. Union members resent the fact that there are so many members of the union competing for so few jobs. Whichever side of the fence you happen to be on, there will always be too many actors applying for too few jobs (that seems to be one of the unwritten rules of the profession). But until you get an opportunity to get into a union, don't let the lack of a union card stop you from looking for work. Nonunion companies abound and are open to young, fledgling performers. In fact, being free to participate in a nonunion film or off-off-Broadway production can be that chance opportunity to get experience and show your stuff. Once you join a union, you will be excluded from working in amateur productions. And if you do, you could jeopardize your union membership.

UNION FACTS AND FEES

Associated Actors and Artists of America (4As) is the national organization under which six separate unions are gathered, including the three dramatic unions that will concern you: Actors' Equity Association (AEA), the Screen Actors Guild (SAG), which now also includes the Screen Extras Guild (SEG), and the American Federation of Television and Radio Artists (AFTRA). (The two other 4A unions are the American Guild of Musical Artists [AGMA], and the American Guild of Variety Artists [AGVA]).

Actors' Equity Association (AEA)

AEA encompasses all professional actors and stage managers in the legitimate theatre throughout the United States. Founded in 1913, it is the oldest of the actors' unions and currently has over 40,000 members. The union's jurisdiction covers Broadway, off Broadway, and off-off-Broadway, business theatre, regional theatre, dinner theatre, summer stock and resident stock, musical theatres, touring companies, children's theatre, and more. "Broadway" encompasses work in theatres in Manhattan that are located in the "Broadway district." "Off Broadway" encompasses work in Manhattan theatres, both commercial and nonprofit, that are not within the Broadway district and have a seating capacity of less than 500. "Off-off-Broadway" encompasses New York City theatres with 100 seats maximum.

You can become a member of Equity in three different ways:

1. By signing a standard Equity employment contract. These contracts include Broadway, League of Regional Theatres (LORT), Stock, and Dinner Theatre. However, union eligibility does not come with every union job. For some Equity jobs covered by the lesser Equity contracts, there are requirements regarding length of employment and wage-earning minimums that have to be met before you can become eligible to join the union. This is obviously a way for the union to control its membership.

2. Actor's Equity Membership Candidate Program. This program, which was begun in 1978, allows you to build up credit toward Equity membership. In order to do this you must land a nonprofessional job at an Equity theatre that offers the program (resident and nonresident stock theatres, dinner theatres, Equity resident theatres, and other theatres around the country that participate in the program), register, and submit the form and a $100 fee to AEA (the fee is credited against your initiation fee). Once you have worked for fifty weeks at an accredited theatre you are eligible to join the union. You have five years after that to join Equity, but all your work has to be through the union.

3. If you are an active member of AFTRA, SAG, SEG, AGMA, or AGVA and have worked under union jurisdiction as either a principle, an "under five," or for three days as an extra, you may join AEA.

The current Equity fees include an initiation fee of $800 and annual dues of $78 paid in two parts. If you are already a member of AGMA or AGVA, the initial fee is $400. In addition, once you are a member of AEA you will pay what are known as "working dues," 2 percent of your gross earnings under Equity contracts.

Certain benefits and protections are provided by Equity contracts (and the other union contracts), such as a guaranteed minimum salary, limits on the hours you may work per day and per week, overtime pay for work beyond specified hours, health insurance, and participation in the union's pension fund.

Screen Actors Guild (SAG)

SAG covers all acting work in film, videotape, television programs, commercials, and MTV, and now includes the Screen Extras Guild. The union was founded in 1933 and has about 75,000 members.

You can join SAG in one of three ways:

1. "Employment as a Principal Performer": Land a principal role or speaking role in a SAG film, TV program, videotape, or commercial.
2. "Employment as an Extra": Work as an extra three times in a SAG film, TV program, videotape, or commercial.
3. If you are already a member of one of the other 4A unions, and have been for at least a year, and have worked as a principal under that union's jurisdiction or as an extra three times, you are permitted to join SAG.

The initiation fee for SAG is currently $862, followed up with dues of $42.50 every six months, and 1½ percent of your earnings under SAG contracts, up to a certain amount.

AFTRA (American Federation of Television and Radio Artists)

AFTRA was founded in 1937 and has about 70,000 members. This union is an open union, which means that you can join simply by applying to your local office and paying the dues, which vary from local to local. AFTRA has jurisdiction over all live and videotaped television programs, radio and television commercials, radio programs, phonograph recordings, and others. You are permitted to work in a job under AFTRA's jurisdiction for 30 days without joining the union.

Actors who have yet to get into a union will sometimes try to circumvent the restrictions of a union casting call because it often seems to be the only way to get to see those people they have to see to get hired. They will fake a union card or borrow a union card to get into an open call. This practice is illegal and risky, and you could be in some trouble if you are found out. Some actors will lie about union affiliation on their résumé. This could be embarrassing because whoever offers you a job will check you out with the union and will definitely not appreciate the deception. Mysterious as the process of getting that first union contract seems, actors manage to do it every year. Once you have joined the union be sure to keep your dues paid up. Familiarize yourself with the rules, attend meetings, and take advantage of the benefits the union offers its members.

Union membership, however, does not guarantee that a job will be waiting for you. Once you join the union you will simply join a different line at tryouts. Now you will be number 191 at an open Equity call for a production that has already been cast, and after six hours of waiting your name will be called, and you will have a two-minute interview with someone (most likely not a producer or

director, but a "representative"), hand in your picture and
résumé for a filing system in the sky, and be out on the
street again in a flash. The unions string a fence between
one line of unemployed actors and another. Here is a very
sensible suggestion from the director of a nonunion summer theatre: "Young performers are advised not to join
Equity until they give it much thought; when they do, they
restrict themselves from applying for many other jobs and
throw themselves in with thousands of other union members looking for work. With so many nonunion dinner
theatres, summer theatres, regional theatres, road tours, et
cetera, there is plenty of work for any actor with a lot of
talent in non-Equity companies. Many of these pay well
and some pay even better than Equity. A good non-Equity
actor can work year-round in his chosen profession."

WHERE THE UNIONS ARE

AEA

NEW YORK
Actors' Equity Association
National/Eastern Office
165 West 46th Street
New York, NY 10036

LOS ANGELES
6430 Sunset Boulevard
Los Angeles, CA 90028

CHICAGO
203 N. Wabash Avenue
Chicago, IL 60601

SAN FRANCISCO
235 Pine Street
San Francisco, CA 94104

SAG

NATIONAL OFFICE
(call for the SAG office in
your area)
7065 Hollywood Boulevard
Hollywood, CA 90028

NEW YORK
1515 Broadway, 44th floor
New York, NY 10036

CHICAGO
307 N. Michigan Avenue
Chicago, IL 60601

SAN FRANCISCO
235 Pine Street
San Francisco, CA 94104

AFTRA

NEW YORK
NATIONAL OFFICE
  (call for the AFTRA
  office in your area)
260 Madison Avenue
New York, NY 10016

CHICAGO
307 North Michigan Avenue
Chicago, IL 60601

LOS ANGELES
6922 Hollywood Boulevard
Hollywood, CA 90028-6128

SAN FRANCISCO
235 Pine Street
San Francisco, CA 94104

FOR THE BEST IN PAPERBACKS, LOOK FOR THE

In every corner of the world, on every subject under the sun, Penguin represents quality and variety—the very best in publishing today.

For complete information about books available from Penguin—including Pelicans, Puffins, Peregrines, and Penguin Classics—and how to order them, write to us at the appropriate address below. Please note that for copyright reasons the selection of books varies from country to country.

In the United Kingdom: For a complete list of books available from Penguin in the U.K., please write to *Dept E.P., Penguin Books Ltd, Harmondsworth, Middlesex, UB7 0DA.*

In the United States: For a complete list of books available from Penguin in the U.S., please write to *Consumer Sales, Penguin USA, P.O. Box 999— Dept. 17109, Bergenfield, New Jersey 07621-0120.* VISA and MasterCard holders call 1-800-253-6476 to order all Penguin titles.

In Canada: For a complete list of books available from Penguin in Canada, please write to *Penguin Books Canada Ltd, 10 Alcorn Avenue, Suite 300, Toronto, Ontario, Canada M4V 3B2.*

In Australia: For a complete list of books available from Penguin in Australia, please write to the *Marketing Department, Penguin Books Ltd, P.O. Box 257, Ringwood, Victoria 3134.*

In New Zealand: For a complete list of books available from Penguin in New Zealand, please write to the *Marketing Department, Penguin Books (NZ) Ltd, Private Bag, Takapuna, Auckland 9.*

In India: For a complete list of books available from Penguin, please write to *Penguin Overseas Ltd, 706 Eros Apartments, 56 Nehru Place, New Delhi, 110019.*

In Holland: For a complete list of books available from Penguin in Holland, please write to *Penguin Books Nederland B.V., Postbus 195, NL-1380AD Weesp, Netherlands.*

In Germany: For a complete list of books available from Penguin, please write to *Penguin Books Ltd, Friedrichstrasse 10-12, D-6000 Frankfurt Main 1, Federal Republic of Germany.*

In Spain: For a complete list of books available from Penguin in Spain, please write to *Longman, Penguin España, Calle San Nicolas 15, E-28013 Madrid, Spain.*

In Japan: For a complete list of books available from Penguin in Japan, please write to *Longman Penguin Japan Co Ltd, Yamaguchi Building, 2-12-9 Kanda Jimbocho, Chiyoda-Ku, Tokyo 101, Japan.*